In the Wake of America's Hannibal:

Tracing Benedict Arnold and the 1775 Expedition to Quebec by Canoe

ALSO BY SAM BRAKELEY

Paddling the Northern Forest Canoe Trail:
A Journey Through New England History

IN THE WAKE OF AMERICA'S HANNIBAL:

TRACING BENEDICT ARNOLD AND THE 1775 EXPEDITION TO QUEBEC BY CANOE

By Sam Brakeley

Lulu Press
Raleigh, North Carolina

Lulu Press, Inc
3101Hillsborough Street
Raleigh, NC 27607

Copyright © 2015 Sam Brakeley.

All rights reserved,
including the right of reproduction
In whole or in part in any form

Cover and Book Design and Layout by Sam Brakeley

Manufactured in the United States of America

ISBN 978-1-329-68151-4

TO DULUTH WING

Who followed in the wake of Benedict Arnold long before I was born

Contents

Preface	3
Author's Note	5
Introduction	7
Historical Background	10
CHAPTER 1 Planning the Trip	13
Interlude: Who Were They?	21
CHAPTER 2 Setting Out	24
Interlude: The Bateaux – Construction and Navigation	31
CHAPTER 3 The Lower Kennebec River	35
Interlude: Their Gear – What They Carried and Wore	46
CHAPTER 4 The Upper Kennebec River	49
Interlude: What Did They Eat?	56
CHAPTER 5 The Great Carrying Place	60
Interlude: In Sickness and In Health	69

CHAPTER 6 The Lower Dead River a. k. a. Flagstaff Lake   72

Interlude: The Expeditions Interactions with American Indians   79

CHAPTER 7 North Branch of the Dead River and the
         Chain of Ponds   82

Interlude: What Did They Do For Fun?   105

CHAPTER 8 The Height of Land   109

Interlude: The Women of Arnold's Army   117

CHAPTER 9 The Arnold River and Lac Megantic   120

Interlude: What Kept Them Going?   129

CHAPTER 10 The Upper Chaudière   133

Interlude: The Quebecois   146

CHAPTER 11 The Lower Chaudière, Etchemin, and
         Saint Lawrence Rivers   150

CHAPTER 12 Quebec City   165

Acknowledgements   169

Notes   171

Bibliography   181

Preface

This is the story of the men and women who followed Benedict Arnold to assault Quebec in 1775 and one individual, myself, who followed their route in 2013. It's about 600 men and women voyaging through the wilderness: their struggles and victories, their challenges and catastrophes, and their eventual arrival on the shores of the St. Lawrence River. Interwoven into this historical narrative is the story of my own journey in 2013, complete with my own challenges and triumphs.

While I followed their route, I certainly did not undergo anything like the trials they endured. The 21st century brought its own set of experiences, however, and my tale complete with modern adventures such as trespassing on hydro-power land, territorial railroad employees and lascivious middle-aged kayakers is not without interest. No one, to my knowledge, has heretofore followed this route in a solo canoe, and so my own journey through rural Maine and Quebec is an integral and exciting part of this story across time.

This book contains two distinct aspects. Each chapter narrates a section of my own trip, taken in August and September 2013. Intermingled within that 2013 narrative is the simultaneous narration of the events that took place over the same geographic section in 1775. These chapters detail our concurrent journeys across time and space.

The second aspect is a series of what I've termed "Interludes". They address not the "what" and "where" of the voyage but instead "how" and "why". Drawing extensively from their journals and diaries, I explore the daily lives of the soldiers on the expedition and answer questions like "What Did They Eat?" and "What Did They Do For Fun?" These Interludes are organized to answer questions as they arise in the narrative but need not be read in order or within the story. They can saved for later, skipped ahead to, or returned to as needed to remind the reader of just what life was like on the trail.

Due to the methods I used to organize this book, time in some cases has necessarily been condensed or elided. While I was always in one place at one time, Arnold and his men were not. They were spread out for miles over the terrain, sometimes with several days' travel between different divisions. In an effort to ease reading and comprehension, I have in most cases treated the army as one unit and organized the journals and narratives by geography, not timeline. As a result of this, you will only infrequently see hard and fast dates. For a more detailed description of where each division and company of the army was at any given time, I recommend to you any of the several academic works on the expedition including Justin Smith's Arnold's March From Cambridge to Quebec; Arthur Lefkowitz's Benedict Arnold's Army; and Thomas Desjardin's Through A Howling Wilderness. They were invaluable to me in my research as I am sure they will be to you.

Finally, while every effort has been made to ensure that everything stated within these pages is indeed fact, errors have possibly been made. These are no one's fault but mine. Please forgive them.

Author's Note

In their journals, the soldiers on the expedition made use of a wide variety of spellings and punctuations when narrating events. To preserve authenticity I keep their unique sense of the English language intact (clarifying where necessary). I've avoided noting their misspellings and grammatical inconsistencies individually within this narrative, however, since to do so would so fill many of their quotations with "sic"s that they would be unreadable. For my own spelling I use 21st century spellings and updated place names. In cases where spelling still seems in flux – some words derived from various American Indian languages are still spelled in various ways – I try to use the most common spelling.

I choose to use the term "American Indian" when discussing indigenous people for several reasons. The phrase appears to be acceptable to the majority of the indigenous peoples of the North American continent. It also preserves continuity throughout the book since journalists use the term "Indian" when describing native peoples.

For Arnold's river craft I use the terms bateau (singular) and bateaux (plural). The words are French for "boat" and "boats" respectively, but in this case denote a specific type of small craft. Again, journalists employ a number of variations on the spelling. For a detailed description of the craft please read the Interlude entitled, "The Bateaux – Construction and Navigation".

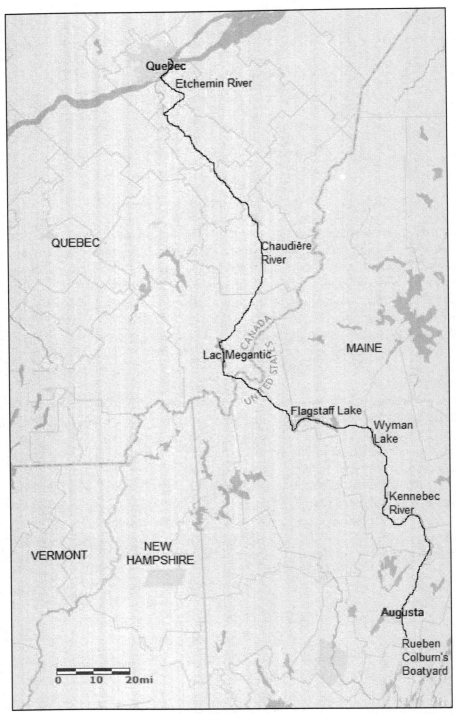
Overview map of author's route tracing Benedict Arnold's 1775 expedition

Introduction

Every canoe trip begins with the germ of an idea. Something; a map, a name, a story, a half-heard radio commercial, anything really, starts a mild unsettling of the stomach and a voice in the back of your head. It asks, "Where's that? I wonder what that looks like. How do I get there?" Excitement builds as you begin to imagine the possibilities of the place. A small point on a map - that pinnacle of green sticking into the blue - can conjure up musings of relaxing by a campfire, bone-tired, surrounded by water on three sides with a breeze gently blowing and the mosquitoes fast asleep. Or the parallel lines marking rapids on a river bring a quickening of the breath: already you're battling whitewater, dodging rocks, and descending ledges as you speed downstream successfully. Regardless of the impetus, you start to ache inside. It starts out gently, just a little bit of a pang in your stomach. But then it starts to grow and soon your whole soul is crying out. You need to discover what is out there, around the river bend. That seed has ballooned into a full-grown need to return to the rivers and woods.

So it was with this trip, although it began surprisingly enough with a novel. Like so many others before me, I discovered Benedict Arnold's march to Quebec in the pages of Kenneth Roberts' <u>Arundel</u>. In that worthy story I found tales of heroic deeds and derring-do, intrigue, rebellion, and love. But most of all, I found a remarkable trip through the wilderness of northern Maine taken by nearly 600 men (although there were many more at the outset as we shall see). They had a destination and a military goal: to capture Quebec City. But the battle wasn't what got my heart beating. What pricked my attention and started that seed growing was the journey. It was the challenge of the woods, the river; the encounter with Mother Nature. The expedition's endurance, tenacity, and strength, against all odds, was remarkable. Day after day, as they fought against the river, sometimes measuring their progress not in miles but in feet, wearing naught but rags by the end and battling starvation and cold, they continued to move inexorably forward. Their perseverance against all odds was simply staggering.

And lo and behold, the story was true. I bought other, non-fiction, books on the subject and Roberts had got it right, down to the smallest detail. Arnold, starting with 1100 men, had traveled nearly 300 miles from present-day Augusta, Maine up the Kennebec and Dead Rivers, across the height of land and Canadian border, and down the Chaudière River to Quebec City in an attempt to take the city from the British near the outset of the Revolutionary War. Their exploits were widely lauded as one of the most ambitious and remarkable operations in military history, not for its military brilliance but for its sheer audacity. "The march itself was a campaign – a campaign against the forest and the flood, against fatigue, sickness, and famine,"[1] noted one historian and another thought it, "not to be paralleled in history."[2] Others, even contemporaries of Arnold, avowed that, "Arnold has made a march that may be compared to Hannibal's or Xenophon's"[3]

In conjunction with <u>Arundel</u>, Kenneth Roberts published some of his research in a book entitled <u>March to Quebec</u>. It was a compilation of many of the journals written by Arnold and other marchers during the event. Roberts had re-discovered and used them during his research and for me, it was a gold mine. I immersed myself in those journals. Some were elaborate in their descriptions, bordering on hyperbole and extravagant in detail as they described their journey through, "hideous swamps and mountainous precipices with the conjoint addition of cold, wet, and hunger not to mention our fatigue – with terrible apprehensions of perishing in this desert,"[4] Others were equally eloquent in their brevity. "Marched 18 miles," reads one journal entry by Moses Kimball for November 6th.[5] Nearby are other entries reading simply "Marched 8 miles Stormed All Day," and "Nothin Remarkable the land very good."[6] This laconicism was no hurdle for my imagination: as I read those brief words every barked shin with muttered curse echoed in my ears and every paddle stroke and ripple went rushing past my mind's eye. Here was adventure in the wilderness at its very best,

And as I read these narratives, that voice in my head, until now only exclaiming in wonder, began to whisper to me. "What if you went on this trip? Wouldn't that be something? You can do it. Go for it!" Roberts states at the beginning of the journals that, "Neither Smith's book nor Codman's [authors of non-fiction works about the expedition], essential as they are as sources, show the peculiarities of the participants in Arnold's great march. Only from the journals themselves can the student gain an understanding of the [marchers],"[7] but to me, even Roberts didn't seem to get it quite right. To go further than simple immersion in the journals seemed necessary, to actually taste the same air, feel the same water, and slog through the same mud that they did appeared necessary to completely understand their journey.

So I did. I set out to replicate the march, "thought to equal Hannibal's over the Alps"[8] and led by the "American Hannibal"[9] himself, Benedict Arnold. Theirs was an ill-fated assault on the British bastion of power in Canada, Quebec

City, which guarded the St Lawrence River. It did not succeed in its ultimate objectives. Nearly 240 years after Arnold and his men, I set out to navigate those same rivers of Maine and Quebec. I hoped to succeed in mine.

Historical Background of the March to Quebec

"An event in the history of the American Revolution...which would deserve and require the talents and genius of a Xenophon"[1] – John Joseph Henry

The thirteen American colonies were in a state of upheaval in 1775. In response to increased war and defense costs due to the recently ended French & Indian War, British Parliament raised taxes on a number of goods including tea, stamps, and sugar. As colonies, the future United States had no elected representatives to Parliament and so the American colonists, infuriated that Parliament was taxing them without adequate representation, struck back. Organizing boycotts and demonstrations, colonists quickly came into conflict with the Queen's red-coated soldiers stationed abroad. Groups like the Sons of Liberty formed to rebel against what was seen as the high-handed dictatorial rule of the mother country. Likewise infuriated at the colonists' perceived ungratefulness, Parliament quartered additional British troops throughout the colonies and increasingly restricted the individual rights of colonists.

Events such as the Boston Tea Party where a group of angry colonists disguised as American Indians dumped tons of tea into Boston Harbor and the Boston Massacre where foolhardy British soldiers fired into an unruly but unarmed crowd only exacerbated the situation and heightened the tension. Extremists calling for total separation from the old country clashed with conservatives encouraging reconciliation while thousands of other colonists tried to decide just which side of the fence they stood on. What had begun as a disagreement was fast becoming a catastrophe for the king and the beginning of a new era for the American continent.

In 1775, everything came to a head. Receiving news that individuals had begun to stockpile arms and ammunition in Concord, Massachusetts, British regulars moved to capture the stores. On a foggy April morning seventy scared but patriotic colonists stared across their muskets over a dewy town green as a phalanx of redcoats faced them. Somebody pulled a trigger and fired the shot heard 'round the world, beginning the American Revolution. British troops and officials holed up in Boston close to their supply lines as militiamen and volunteers raced towards the port city to lay siege. A second and much bloodier encounter on Breed's Hill (later misnamed as The Battle of Bunker Hill) cost the lives of thousands and irrevocably set the opposing sides against each other in a far-ranging and drawn-out war.

Into this melee came George Washington. Appointed by the recently created Continental Congress, he was tasked with commanding the disparate bodies of militias and regular troops. While Congress simultaneously waged war in Boston and petitioned for peace abroad (and refrained from declaring independence for fear of making an irreversible decision), his task was more clear-cut if no less challenging: mold an effective and disciplined army out of the patriotic rabble that had listened to the call to arms and defeat the British Army.

In August of this same year, Benedict Arnold joined the forces outside of Boston and presented himself to Washington. He had a plan to take a group of men through the wilderness of Maine and strike an early blow against the British by taking Quebec City. What exactly Washington thought of brash "Horse Jockey," as his enemies sometimes derisively called him, upon meeting him we cannot exactly know, but the "short, handsome man of a florid complexion [who was] stoutly made,"[2] certainly made an impression on him as he offered his audacious plan to eventually subjugate all of Canada.

Arnold was not the first man to suggest the route through Maine, nor even the first to advocate for the taking of Quebec. The route itself was initially identified for Europeans by none other than Samuel de Champlain who heard about it during his explorations in the area through his interactions with natives. Not one to leave the safety of his sailing ships he explored no further but others took up the cause.

In the late 17th century there were multiple proposals for an expedition heading in the opposite direction, from Quebec towards the colonies, as the French pondered the best way to maintain their foothold on the continent. Later, the British contemplated a maneuver south-to-north to take Quebec from the French. Neither of these plans came to fruition and, since no one seemed particularly interested in taking on the Kennebec or the Chaudière Rivers without government financing, the details of the trip remained scant. As late as 1756 maps were still being produced holding that one could paddle continuously from Maine to Quebec without portaging a height of land.[3]

Additional scraps of information trickled in via missionaries and fur traders but little was known when, in 1761, John Montresor and a small group of men under the British flag set out to explore the Kennebec, Chaudière, and surrounding watersheds. In the course of several weeks he traveled from Quebec to Fort Halifax (now Winslow, Maine on the Kennebec River) and back, nearly starving in the process but meanwhile mapping and taking detailed notes and measurements along the way. By 1775 the Americans had in hand an official copy of his journal and maps. However, due to its military importance, the British had purposefully deleted many of the distances and essential details within. It would be predominantly upon this that Arnold would base his planning of the expedition.

With the siege stagnating around Boston, Washington sought to strike a serious blow to the British before they could organize enough to address colonial resistance with their full resources. Earlier, Arnold, along with Ethan Allen and others had made a daring raid against Fort Ticonderoga on Lake Champlain in May, 1775, solidifying patriotic control of the interior. This became the linchpin of a developing plan to add a fourteenth colony to the rebellion. From there, Washington proposed to strike north along the traditional and well-traveled route down the Richelieu River to Montreal and the St. Lawrence. With Montreal under control, the expeditionary force could then move on to Quebec City and full control of Canada. Washington hoped that with those two cities under the American flag, the whole of French Canada would rise up in support of the revolution and join the American cause.

Early intelligence from Canada supported this notion and indeed, most French-Canadians felt no particular allegiance to the British flag, the French having ceded Canada to the British only a short twelve years previously. General Philip Schuyler was given command of the entire New York theater and, with Ticonderoga as the jumping off point, was ordered to assault Montreal via the Richelieu River. When Arnold came to Washington with his proposal to assault Quebec directly through the Maine woods Washington saw it as an opportune addition to Schuyler's orders. It would both act as a diversionary measure for Schuyler's move north and perhaps be of strategic merit in and of itself if the assault on Quebec went well. Therefore, Washington approved Arnold's timely petition and in late summer of 1775, the expedition to Quebec began to take shape.

Chapter 1: Planning the Trip

"We shall be able to perform the March in twenty Days – the Distance about 180 Miles"[1] –
Benedict Arnold

As I continued to research the expedition, I became more convinced than ever that this was a trip I wanted to take. I wanted to relive their experience and paddle where they had paddled. It took several years and several other canoe trips before I found the time and resources to embark on this one, but once the date was set for late August of 2013, I began to plan and map out the trip in February of the same year. This gave me seven months to plan a trip through populated waters with modern resources and highly detailed maps. Arnold was not so lucky.

. . .

Arnold's prong of the assault was decided upon in August, 1775. On September 8th the army began to leave Cambridge and march towards Newburyport where they would embark on sailing ships and start for Maine. This left far too little time to prepare and plan the expedition but, due to the lateness of the season, it could not be helped.

It was truly a daunting task. For all the audacious planning surrounding the route, very little of it was actually known. Montresor's journal was in hand but again, many of the important mileages and compass bearings were missing. Anecdotal information continued to trickle in, but Arnold needed some concrete intelligence, and fast.

Enter Rueben Colburn, a boat-builder with a shop and mill in the Kennebec Valley who was in Cambridge at the time, advocating for Arnold's same plan for economic reasons. He journeyed back and forth between the Kennebec and Cambridge several times in the months leading up to the expedition's departure, meeting with Arnold and Washington and providing as much intelligence as he could garner. Samuel Goodwin, a New England surveyor familiar with the region, also complied with orders to prepare a map and report of all that was known of the route. These resources along with Montresor's journal would constitute the majority of the information Arnold had to work with before starting out.

. . .

I too tried to discover any intelligence on the route that I could, with more success than Arnold. The Kennebec River is well-treated in paddling guidebooks and maps were easy to find (although all descriptions of the river are laid out in a downstream fashion – it seems that not too many people want to paddle *up* the Kennebec!) I had more trouble with the Chaudière River and found no descriptions of the river's conditions readily available, although my limited understanding of French inhibited my search. But I wasn't too worried – like all rivers, printed materials are only so valuable and are no substitute for on-the-ground scouting. I would take the river as it came.

Like Arnold, I also researched previous travelers. A simple online search brought me to the Arnold Expedition Historical Society (AEHS), a small but dedicated group of individuals devoted to commemorating and researching the trip. They were helpful and supportive but knew of no people who had set out to paddle the whole route in one trip. One or two hints were dropped by somebody faintly remembering an old expedition that had taken on the entire route, but no names or specific resources. They did, however, put me in touch with Duluth Wing who, in the early 1970's, paddled the route in sections with a friend.

Duluth Wing was 85 years old when I called him and told him I wanted to replicate the march, but I would not have known it from talking with him. He was full of energy and could not have been more thrilled that I was setting out to reproduce the trip. "And I live in Eustis," he said, "Right on the way. I have property on the Dead River, and a house near Flagstaff. Come see me when you get to town."

He reminisced about his trips and his paddling partner, but, forty years removed, had little valuable information about the Kennebec or Chaudière – rivers change a lot in four decades. "I've got some information about the Dead River though," he promised. "I've been maintaining some trails near the headwaters that you'll use – when we visit I'll give you the details."

He also mentioned some artifacts that he'd found with a metal detector in the woods. "I'll show you those too – they're in the museum in Stratton. It probably won't be open when you arrive but I've got the key. You'll like them."

But he too, didn't know of anyone who had taken the entire route on in one journey.

Finally, while browsing the internet, I discovered a photocopy of an article in a Maine newspaper, the Bangor Daily News. "Michigan six trace Arnold's trail" it read, and it set my heart pumping.[2] Six men, sponsored by the University of Michigan, of all places, set out to replicate the route in 1973. The article appeared to have caught them in mid-trip, somewhere on the upper

Kennebec, and so no word on whether they had made it or not. Further searching revealed no additional articles online. Who were these guys, why'd they do it, and how did it go? A million questions raced through my head. I had to track them down.

The article included their names, anyways, and the fact that they were at the University of Michigan in the early '70's, so I set about trying to find them. I logged onto a business and social networking site and armed with only that scant information, made some more searches. Surprisingly specific results came back and I emailed four individuals with the correct names and backgrounds, asking if they had, by chance, re-traced Arnold's route in 1973. Hope springs eternal but I wasn't expecting much.

Two of the emails I sent elicited no response and one replied with the fact that he'd never been in a canoe in his life. I was about to head back to the drawing board when I received an email from Frank stating that, "Yes indeed, I was one of the Michigan Six," and, after I mentioned my trouble tracking him down, he gave me the phone number of another member, Parker, who lived only an hour away from me. Brimming with curiosity, I blitzed Frank with a long email overflowing with questions about their trip. He responded with one short question. "Since I live only a couple hours away, would you be interested in meeting up instead of corresponding via email or phone?" Would I be interested in meeting up?! Without a doubt! I called Parker as well and he agreed to join us. We arranged a date for early February of 2013 and, when a blizzard hit, postponed to early April. I couldn't wait.

. . .

Arnold's proposed route up the Kennebec was meant to catch the British unawares and strike a blow to the heart of their Canadian stronghold. Secrecy was an integral part of the plan and several steps were taken to ensure that the British didn't find out about the preparations.

Part of Rueben Colburn's assignment was to send out a scouting party to describe the route as far as Lac Megantic, and to "get particular Information, from those people who have been at Quebec, of the Dificulty attending an Expedition that way, in particular the Number, & length, of the Carrying Places, wheather Low, Dry land, Hills, or Swamp. Also the Depth of Water in the River at this Season, wheather an easy Stream or Rapid."[3] They had a secondary mission of discerning whether or not there were any hostile American Indians or British spies stationed nearby. Two men were duly ordered to travel and although they didn't make it much past the end of the Great Carrying Place, they came back with some disturbing news. An American Indian, Natanis, was living in a small cabin on the Dead River and supposedly spying for the British. Their report also included that "on the Chaudière there was a great Number of Mohawks that would have killed us."[4] All the more reason for Arnold to preserve secrecy and send out some additional scouting parties of his own once he arrived on scene in Maine.

As Arnold gathered stores, arms, and men, the British couldn't help but catch wind of the preparations. Deserters and sympathizers passed back and forth across the siege lines in Boston with surprising regularity and new information was continually being supplied to commanding officers on both sides. But as late as early October, the British thought the intended goal was to be Nova Scotia. It was not until October or early November that the British received what they considered to be confirmation that the real objective was Quebec. This would turn out to be too late to do more than warn Quebec. Reinforcements to the city were not forthcoming and, in a remarkable piece of luck for Arnold, Quebec would be forced to rely on its own resources and garrison when Arnold's men poured forth from the wilderness in November.

. . .

With no British awaiting my own anticipated Quebec arrival and so no secrecy required, Parker, Frank and I met in public at a café in downtown Brattleboro, Vermont. Frank is a middle-aged professor at Amherst College in Massachusetts with thinning hair, glasses, and a tendency to lean way back in his chair as he reminisces. Parker has the appearance of a slightly mad scientist with some similarities to Doc Brown from the movie, *Back to the Future*. He has a quiet, higher-pitched voice and a permanent soft smile. Older than Frank, he was one of two Michigan professors who led the trip, while Frank was one of four graduate students on the journey. Parker lives a simple retired life in Brattleboro where we met for lunch.

As we munched on sandwiches, they recounted their adventures four decades prior while paddling the same route. Between bites of roast beef I learned of battling timber drives and severe pollution – both challenges I did not expect in 2013 – as well as bugs, mud, rain, and high water, all of which I was expecting. They too could not provide me with up to date information on the route, it having been many years since their trip, but that was not what I was looking for. Unlike Arnold, I wasn't desperate for information – I had excellent maps. I just wanted to hear their stories.

"This all began in our hearts and minds," Parker told me. "It was Kenneth Roberts and his novel <u>Arundel</u> that got us interested. We were from the University of Michigan and we felt our liberal education diminished by its primary focus on books and libraries and labs. The humanities could be taught in context."

They decided to expand their horizons and learn on the ground. They used Justin Smith's <u>Arnold's March from Cambridge to Quebec</u> as well as Montresor's journal to research the route and Parker drove the route in advance, meeting up with Duluth Wing like I did (although Duluth would only faintly remember it years later). And on July 30th, 1973 they began. It would take them twenty days to arrive in Quebec.

Parker and Frank had fallen out of touch over the years and hadn't spoken in a while. But as they showed me pictures from their trip, the memories all came flooding back. "Look at us there," cried Frank, referring to their scruffy appearance. "We look like we just pulled off a bank job. Mike [another member] looks like a Mafioso!"

The Kennebec was a challenge for them when they came upon log drives, when timber companies made use of natural forces to get their pulp wood from the forests to the mills. "It looked like a parquet floor," Parker remembered. "There was no way we were getting through it. We had some dicey moments."

And Frank recalled getting stuck near Skowhegan in the gorge. "The Madison Fire Department pulled us out and dried us off. They fed us spaghetti and Crown Royal. Boy, was that good!"

Jerry Gazda was the expedition's photographer, remembered Parker. "When going through rapids he would drop his paddle and hang onto his cameras! We had some close calls there."

Slogging upstream amidst the rain and bugs Frank described as "one of Dante's rings of Hell," but he said it with a fond smile, sitting back and looking heavenward as he recalled the trip. "We've got pictures of us with tape wrapped around our bloody feet from so many blisters."

There were moments of levity, of course. "After a long stretch of rain, Jerry announced that, 'We've got to dry out,'" Parker recounted. "So we did. We all went into a laundromat wearing only our rain gear and sat there while the drying machine did its thing. Later we went to a restaurant and when we sat down, my rain pants rode up past my ankle. There was a big leech there, and I stabbed at it with a cigarette." On the Chaudière River, a Quebec farmer came up to them on the shore and said something in French. The only thing they understood was, "les pommes, les pommes," meaning apples. They stopped and ate apples right off the tree as the farmer looked on with satisfaction. And Frank laughed as he remembered what they ate. "There was no freeze-dried back then. It was all cans. Parker mixed the peanut butter and jelly together into one jar to eliminate weight."

To cross the St. Lawrence, only two paddled (including Frank) while Parker and the other two took a taxi across the bridge – their sixth member had dropped out with one canoe due to injury and then they'd lost a second canoe in a rapid. "I remember trying to decide whether to paddle harder or let-up, to avoid the ocean liners. They were huge! They would have crushed us. But we made it, and climbed the stairs to the Plains of Abraham just like Arnold."

Throughout much of this, I needed to do little prodding. They laughed back and forth, remembering and chatting together as though I wasn't there. Which was fine with me – I just like to hear their stories and memories. It was a trip that I would be taking and to see how much fun they had gotten out of it was powerful. Even had I no plans to recreate the trip, the joy they got from reminiscing would have made this meeting worthwhile.*

I finally asked them what the trip meant to them. Frank grew suddenly thoughtful as he mulled it over. After a moment, he said, "I felt strong for the first time in my life. I had never used my body like that before, and that was when I felt like a man. It had a profound effect on me emotionally." And Parker said, "This trip changed my life's course. The following year I took a trip following Thoreau's canoe travels through Maine, and for many years after I did those trips as part of my curriculum. It changed me as a teacher."

We must have made a sight in that café with pictures, articles, notes and journals spread across the table as the place rang with our hilarity. Lunch over, we parted ways but with promises to reconvene in October once my own journey was done. This meeting was a powerful incentive to head out on this trip and my preparations took on new enthusiasm.

· · ·

Planning a trip for 1100 men was no easy task. There were a thousand details to see to. Not only did Arnold need information and maps but he needed men, boats, equipment, arms, food, medicine, and all the other pieces that make up an expedition. The ever helpful Rueben Coburn was dispatched back to Pittston to begin constructing "Two hundred light battoos capable of carrying six or seven men each with their provisions & Baggage,"[5] along with oars, paddles and setting poles. He was also ordered, "to bespeak all The Pork, and Flour, you can from the inhabitants upon the River Kennebeck,"[6] as well as beef and other edibles. Coburn would also join the expedition for the first several weeks to help maintain the boats in good, working order (a decision that would prove providential since we will see the bateaux required numerous repairs).

In Cambridge, Arnold concerned himself with finding men for the expedition. He wanted only willing bodies and therefore was looking for "volunteers as are active woodsmen & well acquainted with bateaux, so it is recommended that none but such will offer themselves for this service."[7] Both Washington and Arnold wanted nobody on the expedition who didn't want to be there themselves.

---

*Parker and Frank's trip ended up having eerie similarities to Arnold's own march. One member broke his kneecap on the Dead River and went home, near where Enos retreated homewards with 400 men. Since they were down to five men, they left one canoe at the border where Arnold abandoned his remaining bateaux, and wrecked another at Grand Falls when an unforeseen rise in water floated their boats away in the middle of the night (Arnold wrecked a few of his precious remaining bateaux here too). Parker and Frank's group split then, two men paddling and three walking along the shore just like Arnold was forced to do in 1775.

Tents, blankets, clothes, cooking utensils and other gear came from the quartermaster and Dr. Isaac Senter signed on as the expedition surgeon. He would be one of many who left a journal, including Arnold himself. The supply list of course included arms and ammunition, and their baggage even included the musical necessities for four drummers and two fifers who joined.

Yet after all of research and the hundreds of minutiae that Arnold tried to anticipate and see to, he had no idea just what they were in for. Partway into the expedition, he was able to write to Washington that, "Our march has been attended with an amazing deal of fatigue. I have been much deceived in every Account of our Rout[e], which is longer, and has been attended with a Thousand Difficulties I never apprehended..."[8]

Regardless, by September 8th the army was as ready as it was ever going to be, and time was growing short. They mustered on Cambridge Common, issued gear and began the march to Newburyport, Massachusetts. From there, they would embark on ships to sail to Rueben Colburn's boatyard on Kennebec River to embark on the march "not to be paralleled in history"[9]

. . .

While not outfitting 1100 men, I felt my own preparations to be no less complicated. Accounting for everything from matches to pocket knife to toothbrush and toothpaste, I tried to cross all the 'T's and dot all my 'I's to make sure I too, was ready to take the trip to Quebec. When preparing for any canoe trip, my technique is to walk through a typical day in my head and think of every possible tool I might need that day, then check it off the list. "So I wake up, unzip my sleeping bag – check – roll off my sleeping pad – check – and unzip my tent – check. Build a fire with matches – check – and axe – check. Cook breakfast with a pot – check and spoon – check. Brush my teeth with toothbrush and toothpaste – check, check." And so on. It's an imperfect system but it usually works for me. I then go through an extra list of items not required every day: spare paddle, portaging gear, medical kit, and so on to make sure I've got all those necessaries as well.

For food, if I'm guiding a group then I plan out every meal meticulously, but when by myself, I like to bring ingredients: rice, beans, cheese, fresh vegetables, oatmeal, sugar, raisins, bread, peanut butter etc. Then I can make any combination of things I want. Peanut butter and jelly is fairly ubiquitous but if I'm in the mood for a Thai-style meal then I can add peanut butter to the rice. Do I feel like grilled cheese for dinner? Sure I can make that too. And if it means I'm having a bean sandwich for the last meal before I resupply again, that's okay. Besides, having the benefit of secure civilization along the entire length of this route, I never needed carry more than a couple of days' worth of food at one time.

With everything together, I made one final check and then packed it all up. To my regular paddling I gear I added a copy of Kenneth Roberts' March to Quebec. I planned to read the compiled journals within each night, lulling myself to sleep with the narratives of the men. Where I paddled on any given day, I could then that night read their journals describing their own journey over the same ground nearly 250 years prior. It would be a wonderful way to end each day.

My own journey towards Colburn House would be by car but I like to think that I felt a similar sense of anticipation as I packed and repacked my gear on August 21, 2013. As Abner Stocking, a private on the expedition, narrates, "We were all high spirits, intending to endure with fortitude, all the fatigues and hardships, that we might meet with in our march to Quebec."[10] My sentiments exactly, and I went to sleep late that night, too wrought up with anticipation to rest well.

Interlude: Who Were They?

"I panted to partake in the glory of defending my country"[1] – George Morison

The Continental Army led by General George Washington was a motley rabble when he took the helm in 1775. One of his most pressing tasks was to mold the disorganized masses that had flocked to Boston at the first gunshot into not only a well-dressed, well-disciplined army but also one that could be an effective fighting force against the greatest military in the world. Nothing less would even give the British a run for their money. So what was George Washington's clay with which to mold and why did they join?

Individuals from all strata of society answered the siren call to arms. But most predominant were the lower levels of society. Wealthier farmers and craftsmen simply had too much at stake in their families, property, and careers to lay it all on the line for an army that few felt had a chance. Unless drafted or pressed, many of the wealthier men stayed home. It fell to the poorer laborers and itinerant workers to make up the majority of the ranks. These men joined, not only for the initial bounty but also hoping for square meals, regular pay, and a roof over their heads. As historian Michael Stephenson says, "Men joined because it was the best deal on offer in a world that did not offer them any really good deals."[2] But this deal too was not always what it seemed to be and men did go without food, pay and shelter, sometimes for months. Rum or other liquor was also a part of the daily ration – another incentive for many – and men were not loath to partake of that libation. Boredom, disenchantment, and booze all led to drunkenness and desertion, and Washington quickly had his hands full disciplining his new troops. He used the threat of lashing, public humiliation and even execution (sometime followed by last minute reprieves as we shall see) to keep them in line, with varying degrees of success.

Other troops joined for a sense of adventure. With few prospects beyond dreary hard labor while fighting for your next meal, the chance to participate in as big an adventure as a war was not something to be shunned. Recruiters downplayed the work and hazards and up-played the adventure and rum. John Henry, a rifleman, described himself as "unconscious of danger, and animated by a hope of applause from [my] country."³ He was merely looking to participate in an adventure and win some renown. And at age 16, he simply was not equipped with a developed frontal lobe to worry about the consequences. While casualty rates were high in the army and disease rampant, Henry and other recruits were not necessarily aware of this. They entered the army as a lark, frequently signing their name while drunk (a favorite tactic of recruiters), and prepared to embark on greatest escapade of their lives.

Finally, men joined from a sense of patriotism. George Morison, a private, stated that, "from my youth I had felt an ardent attachment to liberty."⁴ While this may partially be grandstanding for his audience, it does describe the sentiments felt by many. There was a genuine sense of outrage at the British for their approach to relations with the colonies and it was from a sense of patriotic enthusiasm that many others answered the call.

It was these last two reasons, adventure and patriotism, that drew some of the wealthier strata of society. Officers were frequently of a more landed background than many of the enlisted men and usually had property and status within their communities, although often not high enough to please the class-conscious British. "One major was a blacksmith, another a hatter; of their captains there was a butcher, a tanner, a shoemaker, a tavern-keeper etc. yet they all pretended to be gentlemen,"⁵ harped one British officer. Men elected their officers in the Continental Army and they frequently chose local leaders from the towns back home. But, at least according to the British, this did not make them gentlemen. They were, however, a class above the privates and this helped, at least marginally, to maintain the distance between ranks that Washington and his dedication to discipline so fervently hoped for.

The army that followed Arnold to Quebec was a microcosm of the Continental Army. Perhaps, because both Washington and Arnold required that they all be volunteers, they were more fervent in their patriotism and less inclined to dissolution and desertion but discipline problems arose nonetheless. However, by and large, it was a dedicated group of men, certainly fired with a sense of adventure, who set out for Quebec in early September of 1775.

Like any expeditionary force it had a sampling of the army as a whole. In addition to the enlisted soldiers (who carried muskets), non-commissioned officers, and officers, there were three companies of riflemen, four drummers and two fifers, a surgeon, a chaplain, and at least nine American Indians to act as guides, scouts, and messengers. The detachment also included several gentlemen volunteers (unpaid assistants to lesser officers who sought by their own performance to earn commissions*), at least four women who were following their husbands to Quebec and at least one black man. Several dogs rounded out

---

* One of whom was Aaron Burr – later infamous for his own alleged traitorous actions.

the bunch.

Our journalists, upon whom we rely for first-hand information, fall into these same categories. There is Benedict Arnold himself, of course. Arnold was a merchant in Connecticut before the war. Major Return J. Meigs was a merchant and occasional counterfeiter from Connecticut. Captain Henry Dearborn also left an account and had just begun a medical practice when he joined Arnold. Captain Simeon Thayer was a peruke-maker from Massachusetts. The surgeon, Dr. Isaac Senter, was from New Hampshire. John Joseph Henry was only sixteen when he joined and would later become a judge in Pennsylvania. Caleb Haskell was a sailor and fifer from Massachusetts. Other privates who left accounts included James Melvin, Moses Kimball, George Morison, Abner Stocking, Simeon Fobes, William Dorr, Ebenezer Tolman, Francis Nichols, Mathias Ogden, John Topham, Ephraim Squier, and a journal known only as written by 'Provincial' because his name is unknown (see notes for source locations). Privates varied as much in their occupations as the officers did. All in all they come from a wide variety of backgrounds with varying experiences.

Journals include everyone from the commander, Arnold, to the lowliest private as well as the surgeon (Senter) and a gentleman volunteer (Ogden). During the march, the men were split into four divisions for ease of travelling and journalists come from all four divisions. One journalist, Simeon Fobes, even makes the journey twice. He escaped British imprisonment after the failed assault on Quebec and retraced the route with two others to arrive back home in New England. Altogether, they offer a unique and unparalleled view of the Revolutionary War, as few events have had as many narratives written about it as has Arnold's march to Quebec.

Chapter 2: Setting Out

"We were all in high spirits intending to endure with fortitude, all the fatigues and hardships, that we might meet with in our march to Quebec"[1] – Abner Stocking

My journey to Rueben Colburn's boatyard was much simpler than Arnold's. With the canoe – a 16' Old Town Penobscot – strapped to the roof of the car, I threw my gear in the back, climbed in, and took off. My girlfriend rode in the passenger seat – she was my Subaru's ticket back home, and the two of us spent 3 hours driving to Portland, Maine where we would spend the night with my aunt and uncle (a convenient break in the drive and a chance to see family) before Elizabeth would drop me off the next morning at Colburn's.

It was an uneventful car ride. Elizabeth, well known for her ability to fall asleep within five minutes of departure, was gently snoring before we turned onto the highway. I turned the radio on, prepared to enjoy my final hours of music before I took a break from it for a couple of weeks. One thing I am adamant about when I hit the woods to play is that I experience the woods. Today's migration towards piped in music as background for all outdoor activity disappoints me. Whether it be skiing, hiking, running, or paddling, I empathically refuse to wear head phones to drown out nature's voice with imported sound. So I danced to Steely Dan and the Moody Blues one last time as Elizabeth snoozed and we set out on one of two driving legs to get to the put-in.

· · ·

Arnold also had two legs in his journey to get to Colburn's, but instead of each leg being a simple matter of hours, his approach was a complicated, multi-day affair. The men gathered in Cambridge and began their march northwards by foot on September 11th. To preserve secrecy and "for the more convenient marching and lodging,"[2] they split into multiple small groups. Taking between two and three days, these smaller bodies stopped in towns along the way including Lynn, Ipswich, Beverly and Salem. Once gathered again in Newburyport, Massachusetts, they would embark on ships to sail the rest of the way to Maine.

Newburyport was "a very agreeable place,"[3] according to Dr. Senter, and the officers and some of the men were able to find indoor lodging. The rest set up tents in or near town. On September 17th, the men paraded across Newburyport green and, according to Ebenezer Wild, "our men appeared very well and in good spirits and made a grand appearance."[4] With his typical hyperbole, George Morison concurred with Wild, touting the men's zeal and courage as they embarked. "[The soldiers'] heroic labor, their love of glory, their steady attachment for each other, constitute their health and happiness, keep up a constant glow of soul, which the indolent and luxurious never feel."[5] Clearly, omens were interpreted to be in favor of a successful march and the outlook was positive as they prepared for the second half of the trip to Pittston and Colburn's boatyard.

Their second leg was only slightly less enjoyable. From Newburyport they embarked on a number of ships to sail as far up the Kennebec as was feasible. After a brief delay as the crew of one ship, the *Swallow,* futilely tried to disengage their ship from where it was stuck on a sand bar, they transferred the soldiers to other ships and continued on. Described as "dirty coasters & fish boats"[6] by Simeon Fobes, this was no magnificent full-fledged battle fleet but it certainly sufficed as effective troop transports along the coast. Fortunately no British ships were nearby so their lack of battle-readiness and armaments was a non-issue. They did have some stormy waters, however, and Dr. Senter, with tongue in cheek, wrote that night in his journal that the volatile seas "occasioned most of the troops to disgorge themselves of their luxuries so plentifully laid in ere we embarked."[7]

It took only slightly more than a day to sail along the Maine coast to the mouth of the Kennebec but there the ships were forced to pick their way in and amongst the many islands that dot the outlet of the big river. Indeed, two ships mis-read the multiple channels and went up nearby Sheepscot River before discovering their mistake and rejoining the rest of the fleet in Merrymeeting Bay, a large inland body of water just several miles up the Kennebec. By September 21st the first ships had managed to achieve Colburn's shipyard in Pittston and the remainder rendezvoused there the next morning. The area became a frenzy of packing and re-packing as the men transferred gear, stores, and arms from ships to bateaux. They had reached their jumping off point.

. . .

Ironically, Arnold overnighted indoors far more frequently early in the trip than I would. Whereas locals would likely have looked askance at a request from me to put up at their house for the night, Arnold lived in a different age in a different situation. Hospitality of this kind was a given in the 18th century and it was an honor to house an officer such as Arnold for the night, especially during wartime. Even in 1775 the lower Kennebec was not a wilderness and for its final descent the eighty or so miles from Norridgewock to the sea its banks were dotted with farms and houses. North of Norridgewock it became the unknown wilderness so anticipated, but below that the region had been more or less settled. Officers made use of these homes and Arnold himself managed to stay under a roof until October.

But I left running water and heat behind me in Portland. Chuck and Diane fed and housed me, treating me to a delicious home-cooked meal and a warm bed. The next morning, August 22nd, we sat down to cereal, scones and bagels with fresh orange juice and coffee. The scones in particular hit the spot and I savored them, knowing as I did that it'd be oatmeal, oatmeal and more oatmeal for many mornings to come.

"Are you going to get enough to eat, Sam?" Diane was worried about me.

"Don't you fret, Aunt Diane. I'll be fine" One thing I make sure to never be short of is food.

Uncle Chuck was worried about black flies and mosquitoes. "What kind of bug dope did you bring?"

"Nothing, Uncle Chuck. I'll just paddle fast enough that they won't be able to keep up with me," I joked. But it was the truth. I hadn't packed any. Bug spray only works to keep off occasional, indolent mosquitoes. It doesn't work on dedicated swarms. If the bugs were bad enough that it became irksome, I had a mosquito net packed.

Elizabeth and I made our farewells and were on the road by 8 AM. It took us slightly over an hour to make the drive to what is now known as the Major Rueben Colburn House, property of the State of Maine and headquarters of the Arnold Expedition Historical Society. I too had reached my put-in and while not as effusive as George Morison, I was ready to go.

· · ·

At Colburn's shipyard, the men beheld their newly built bateaux "all Lying on Shore ready to receive our detachment."[8] They left their ships, loaded the bateaux, and headed upstream. The expedition was simply picking up the boats from Colburn here; they would organize thoroughly at Fort Western (now Augusta, Maine) only six miles upstream. Organizationally, we'll consider their jumping off point as Fort Western since this was where final arrangements for their trip took place. With no further arrangements needed upstream, my own jumping off point was there at Colburn House.

One of the surprising facts of this river expedition was that some of the men walked to Quebec. While many were indeed paddling and dragging the bateaux filled with gear, many others were forced to make their way along shore. From Colburn House to Fort Western and beyond to Fort Halifax there was a rough road but soon afterwards the walkers were forced to bushwhack the rest of the way. The constructed bateaux could not fit the entire army and all its gear and equipment so many marched alongside the Kennebec as best they could.

The six miles from Colburn House to Fort Western are flat with only a gentle current but the men likely struggled as many attempted to pilot their bateaux for the first time. If they timed it correctly, they would have had the incoming tide to help them along and while there may have been a mishap or two, the first miles would be some of the easiest. Few of the journalists comment on their first bateaux experiences but there was doubtless a breaking-in period. Arnold had hoped to sail in the ships all the way to Western but low water forced him to stop short and embark via bateau and on foot from Colburn's.

At Fort Western Arnold led a massive effort to finally begin the trip. Remember that Arnold was relying upon scant information: some from Montresor's incomplete journal and some more up-to-date data from Samuel Goodwin's scouting and map. To supplement this with immediate first-hand knowledge, several scouting parties were dispatched to strike out ahead, obtain intelligence, mark portages, and among other orders, kill the supposed British spy Natanis. One journalist, John Joseph Henry, was among them (his reminiscences will be organized here geographically along with the other journalists).

The remainder was split up into four divisions. The riflemen were grouped together under Daniel Morgan as a sort of light infantry. They would be the vanguard and help to scout and clear portages. Christopher Greene would command the second, uniquely named Return Meigs the third, and Roger Enos the final division. Splitting the men into four divisions would facilitate travel and camping arrangements and prevent bottlenecks at portages. Daniel Morgan, charged some scouting duties and with clearing portages traveled lighter while Enos' division, with the assumption that they would have an easier time over previously cleared portages and a well-marked route, was given a larger portion of the rations. They would then send forward provisions as needed by advance divisions as the march progressed. Also marching with Enos would be Rueben Colburn and some of his builders, enlisted for the first part of the journey to provide any needed repairs to the boats.

A makeshift encampment sprung up around Fort Western on that first night, abuzz with more excitement than the old fort had seen in a long time. Fort Western was built during the French & Indian War but had since fallen into disrepair and was now only used as a private residence and trading post. So while some were able to find shelter indoors, many threw up tents on the grounds surrounding the fort. As night fell on September 24th, hundreds of cooking fires twinkled around the fort and anticipation was certainly in the air as the men looked forward to the trip. Tradition holds that a large banquet was given for the army but as no journalists mention it, it seems unlikely. Henry describes the feeling at Western as "unconscious of danger, and animated by a hope of applause from their country,"[9] and talk around the campfires no doubt concerned the coming adventure and challenges.

That evening, however, an event occurred to put a pall over the mood. As Dearborn narrates, "This evening a very unhappy accident happened...some warm words produced a quarrel and one McCormick being turned out of the House soon after discharged his Gun into the House and shot a man Thro."[10] The struck man died and the accused, John McCormick, was duly convicted and sentenced to hang. Arnold commuted the sentence, however, and McCormick was sent back to Washington for final disposition. It was not how Arnold had hoped to begin northwards.

It would take several days at Western before everything was in preparation, but by September 25th, 1775 the first division under Daniel Morgan and comprised of his three rifle companies was able to set off after the scouting party (who had left the day before). The three remaining divisions of Greene, Meigs and Enos followed, spacing their departures out by a day each although Enos, tasked with organizing all the final details, was not able to leave Western until September 30th. Arnold left Western on the 29th in a birch bark canoe which he quickly switched to a dugout due to leakage. By traveling light he was able to move back and forth between his divisions relatively quickly. It had taken a monstrous amount of effort to even set off, but finally, the march to Quebec had begun in earnest.

.   .   .

When I arrived at Colburn House on August 22nd, 2013, no bateaux waited for me. Colburn himself was long gone and indeed, not a soul was present. It was a beautiful day with the sun shining and the birds chirping, but I would have no send-off party besides Elizabeth (not that I am denigrating her send-off capabilities – she is more than capable of fueling a one-woman party). I had tried to get someone from the Arnold Expedition Historical Society to be present but to no avail, so while the Society has done a wonderful job of preserving his house and workshop, I was not able to enter. We were reduced to peering through windows – the house was set up as a museum and the workshop appeared largely empty. A few minutes of nosing around determined that I'd have to come back later to get the full experience.

While Arnold took days, I took minutes to organize at Colburn House. Stuffing my groceries in my bag and strapping my paddles into the canoe, I portaged down to the water's edge following a mowed path before forcing my way through the final feet of shrubs to the water. The tide was out (I wanted its help to paddle the first miles) so I slogged across 100 feet of mud before reaching the water. Elizabeth stayed dry and took pictures from the shore. I clowned briefly, setting my boat in the mud and aping paddling attempts.

"That's not going to work, honey!" Elizabeth shouted. "Do you want me to show you how to paddle?"

This was a running joke between us – the last time we went paddling together we flipped in a small rapid which I continue to adamantly blame on her.

"Like this?" I replied, moving the canoe into water deep enough to float in.

"You're doing great," she laughed. "You'll be there in no time now!"

She took a couple more pictures, blew me a kiss good-bye, and I was off. Quebec or bust.

As in 1775, the first miles between Colburn's house and Fort Western were easy. With the tide at my back I fairly flew and it took only slightly more than an hour to reach Augusta, Maine. The banks were lined with houses (remember, even in Arnold's day this stretch of river was fairly settled although certainly not to the extent that it is now in the 21st century). I spotted a golden eagle high in the branches of an oak tree, calling across the river to another. Being downstream of a city, I was surprised to find little obvious evidence of pollution or debris – no oil slicks slid across the surface of the Kennebec and the banks were relatively clear of trash. That would change as I entered downtown Augusta, however, where the banks of the river showed long-term human impact in the form of ancient wooden and cement retaining walls and piers and debris began to accumulate along the edges.

As I neared the center of the city, a large imposing structure loomed on the east side. It was the Kennebec Arsenal, built in the first half of the 19th century in response to border disputes with Great Britain. Later a mental hospital, it has fallen into disuse though the grounds are still maintained. I dragged the canoe on shore and poked around but there was little to see that I hadn't seen from afar. Mostly it seemed to act as a place to jog or walk dogs for locals. But it did have a magnificent lawn, well-kept, and I sat down on the hillside looking out over the river to rest my shoulders for just a minute.

They didn't seem to need it. They did ache a little from paddling, but their other burdens were quickly sliding away. Just a few hours into the trip, the worries of what now seemed like a prior life began to evaporate. No more worrying about business, scheduling, e-mail, bills, or the other cares of every-day existence. I was on the river now. There is nothing so freeing as a long trip, and for the next two weeks, I could afford to ignore my cares. I felt like I was a separate human being, able to look at my other self with a little bit of humor and pity. I had left the other Sam behind – the one who had to deal with all those considerations. This Sam, the one I was right now, could live in the present and enjoy the river and the trip. It was certainly a wonderful feeling and after a minute I jauntily returned to my boat, ready to see what was up ahead on the river. After all, that was the only thing that mattered.

Continuing on, I finally spotted the remains of Fort Western just before crossing under the Rte. 100 bridge in Augusta. Clambering up the steep slope through Japanese knotweed (a ubiquitous invasive species that is the scourge of riverbanks and road edges), I skirted the old palisade that guarded the blockhouse and was about to enter when I was stopped short by a voice.

"Can you sign-in over here, please?" An older woman dressed in 18th century garb was standing outside a small visitor center at the entrance.

"Sure," I said. "I just want to poke around for a bit."

"I'm sorry. We only allow people inside if they are part of a tour. The next one will be in fifteen minutes."

Surprised, I declined. The blockhouse appeared to be most of the tour along with some cannons parked nearby. I was neither interested in waiting for a tour nor in paying the entrance fee so I chatted briefly with her and another man – also costumed – before returning. Thanks but no thanks.

The bank was steep enough that it was closer to a controlled fall than a hike to get back down to the river but I managed and, as I dipped my paddle once more, realized that from here on out both Arnold and I would be on the same path in the same type of watercraft. "Here goes nothing," I said to myself and pulled with renewed vigor.

Interlude: The Bateaux – Construction and Navigation

"Could we then have come within reach of the villains who constructed these crazy things, they would have fully experienced the effects of our vengeance."[1] – George Morison

One of the most controversial aspects of Arnold's trip, both then and now amongst historians was the boats they used, known as bateaux. Bateaux are shallow, flat-bottomed boats and can be built to a number of sizes. While no one is quite sure of the size of Arnold's boats, we can assume they were somewhere in the neighborhood of twenty to twenty-five feet long and at least several feet wide. When ordering them from Colburn, Arnold specified that they be "capable of carrying six or seven men each with their provisions and baggage – the boats to be furnished with four oars, tow paddles, and two setting poles each."[2] We can be sure, however, that those used were smaller than he anticipated since upon arrival he immediately ordered twenty more built and a number of journalists comment on their smaller than expected size.

Their diminutive dimensions were a result of the short amount of time that Rueben Colburn had to construct them. He received his orders in Boston in September and therefore had only a little more than two weeks before Arnold's arrival at his workshop in which to construct the craft. It can only be because of his excellent work ethic and organizational abilities that he was even able to construct them at all. But this extremely short time frame also meant that seasoned wood could not be used. A boat builder in northern Maine simply would not have that much dried lumber available at any given time and so many of the boats were necessarily built using freshly cut timber. Dr. Isaac Senter stated that "The bateaux were made of green pine boards which made them somewhat heavy,"[3] and estimated their weight at "not less than four hundred pounds."[4] He called them "little better than common rafts."[5] Arnold himself concurred and reported to Washington upon inspection that they were "smaller than the directions given and very badly built."[6]

When in Portland my aunt had challenged me on my decision to use a canoe. "You know you're cheating, Sam, right?" she half-jokingly accused. "Arnold used bateaux. Why aren't you doing the same?" Apparently she had made some inquiries of her own regarding the trip.

"A bateau?! Aunt Diane, I'm not crazy," I protested. "There is no earthly reason why I should. Those things weighed hundreds of pounds and were not the most maneuverable. The only reason they used them was because they had so much gear. Besides, Arnold used a canoe!"

Indeed several canoes made the journey along with the hundreds of bateaux. The scouting party led by Lieutenant Archibald Steele with John Henry among it traveled to nearly the Canadian border and back to the Great Carrying Place in canoes. As stated before, Arnold himself made much of the journey in a canoe – paddled by experienced American Indians – to facilitate his easy movement between disparate divisions. And others used canoes briefly as well: Dearborn used one on the Chaudière River while the remainder of the army walked because he was too sick to march, and the entire army used an eclectic mix of dugouts, birchbark canoes and other craft to cross the St. Lawrence. If Arnold had had the choice, he no doubt would have chosen canoes for the whole of the expedition. But the amount of gear and arms required by an invading army forbade the use of such small craft, so bateaux it would be. It's actually remarkable that even these sufficed – armies simply did not move by such small craft in the 18th century. So I felt secure in my decision to use a canoe for the journey and not one of the "crazy things."

Colburn could not help the hurried construction of the bateaux, which Arnold fully realized, so he was detailed to follow the expedition to make any and all required repairs along the way. Some of the journalists railed against their constructers, saying "Did they not know their doings were crimes, exposing [America's] defenders to additional sufferings and to death?"[7] But this was likely posturing for their anticipated reading audience since Colburn was right there, working alongside the army. They could have voiced their concerns to Colburn himself, had they so chosen. In the event, they knew as well as Arnold that it couldn't be helped.

Bringing Colburn and his crew along would prove to be a highly necessary decision for the boats did require frequent repairs to be kept in operating order. Journalists frequently narrate a common chore where, "We haul'd up our bateaus and caulk'd them as best we could."[8] Senter records partway up the Kennebec that, "by this time many of our bateaux were nothing but wrecks, some stove to pieces, &c,"[9] and at Fort Halifax, only a few miles into the trip, he wrote that, "my bateau had arrived at the fort, in such a shattered condition, that I was obliged to purchase another."[10] Boat repair would be a constant on the trip.

There was a steep learning curve for the men tasked with paddling the bateaux upstream. While Washington had requested that only men familiar with boating volunteer for the expedition, it quickly became clear that much of the army was novices when it came to bateaux navigation. "The men in general, not understanding bateaux have been obliged to wade and haul them for more than halfway up the river," reported Arnold in a letter back to Washington.[11] Aaron Burr in a letter home wrote, "Imagine to yourself 200 Battoes managed by men – two thirds of whom had never been in one."[12] It would be trial by fire for, with winter coming on and a steep Maine river ahead, there was little time to dawdle and practice.

      The Kennebec did not allow for a grace period of acclimation. "Not once in the whole course of of the passage from Fort Halifax to the head of the Kennebeck was there an occasion for rowing," complained Morison, and indeed lining or dragging the boat was sometimes the only recourse for advancement.[13] "While one took the bow another kept hold of the stern to keep her from upsetting or filling with water," elaborated Abner Stocking, and each bateau had a painter, or bow line, attached to the front to ease lining.[14] Other techniques included hard paddling or poling (using a long wooden pole with metal tip to push off the river bottom for forward propulsion) to move upstream. Each technique brought its own challenges and fatigues and sometimes progress could only be measured in inches as they fought to navigate a particularly challenging set of rips or rapids.

      Portaging brought with it a whole new set of challenges. The boats were weighty and the food, stored in large wooden casks, was no easy burden itself. The bateaux were transported one of several ways. Some crews chose to place two handspikes underneath the boats, carrying them with four men along the portage. "Our progress under these immense burthens was indeed slow, having to lay them down at the end of every few rods to rest," narrates a journalist and one suspects that the hastily cleared portages did not offer any easy traveling or respite from the labor.[15] Anyone who has carried a large, uncooperative object with others can picture the awkward push and pull as each individual stumbles along with their own gait while attempting to step in time with the others. Other groups tried inverting the boats, but four hundred pounds is quite a burden for shoulders. As Simeon Fobes describes, "four men would take one on their shoulders and march along, the edge of the boat being somewhat sharp, pressing very painfully on the flesh."[16]

      Portaging techniques for the provisions were just as varied. Some chose to sling the barrels with ropes and carry them with several men, fully loaded. Others, like Abner Stocking, chose a different method. "Our pork we took from the barrels and strung it on poles," he tells us.[17] One has trouble picturing two men, marching through the woods, with vast quantities of meat strung on a pole without chuckling just a little bit.

      Regardless, the bateaux were a sore spot – literally and figuratively – for the men and they vented much frustration on them. It could not be helped, however, and most managed to make do.

      I was thankful to have a canoe. My gear and food I kept in a durable, waterproof bag with shoulder straps. It sat in the bottom of the boat while paddling and was strapped to my back for portages. The canoe I balanced on my *shoulders with the help of some pads strapped to the center thwart and a tumpline – a leather strap configured in such a way as to spread some of the weight from my shoulders to my back and neck as well. Odd remnants of gear such as water bottles, maps, and axe I strapped inside the canoe before inverting it over my head. In this manner I was able to carry everything in one trip on portages relatively easily (whereas Arnold's men would sometimes take seven or eight trips back and forth over the same ground to accomplish the transport of all their gear). It was a distinct advantage, permitted me only by the advancements that three and half centuries of invention have created. For all the outdoor gear innovators out there, I am thankful.*

Chapter 3: The Lower Kennebec River

"The water in many places being so shallow that we were often obliged to haul the boats after us through rocks and shoals, frequently up to our middle and over our heads in the water; and some of us with difficulty escaped being drowned."[1] – Abner Stocking

Leaving Augusta and Fort Western behind, I paddled northwards, finally feeling like I was on Arnold's trail. The first six miles from Colburn House to Augusta were the warm-up, for both Arnold and myself. Now it was time to make some miles.

The stretch of water between there and Fort Halifax at Waterville, ME was surprisingly uninhabited. Large distances went by without a visible sign of civilization on either bank (although construction and traffic noises filtered through the trees from nearby roads). Large boulders speckled the shallow waters near shore, stained white by the sun, and the water sparkled invitingly. I gave in to the feeling and practiced my whistling (I can barely get a shrill, toneless noise out, but I like to try. Besides, with a tune playing in my head along with it, it sounds good to me, and I'm the only one that matters). It was a pleasant paddle along what I had expected to be an unpleasant section of river.

As I was rounding one river bend, where no houses or roads fronted the river, I spotted a flash of movement. Ahead of me on the right rested a large, shirtless man on an oversized rock. He was reading a newspaper, and as he turned the page, the movement caught my attention. I paddled up to him, but for the life of me could not figure out how he had managed to arrive there. Unbroken trees lined both banks. Overweight, half-naked men don't just fall from the sky, however, so he must have walked in from somewhere.

"You know, in the thirty-one years I've been living on this river, I've never seen anybody going upstream," he greeted me.

"First time for everything," I nonchalantly responded, secretly pleased to be in so select a group though I suspected he hadn't spent all thirty-one years on the lookout for upstream paddlers. I still didn't know how he had got where he was.

"Where you headed?"

"Quebec City," I said, watching carefully to see what his reaction was.

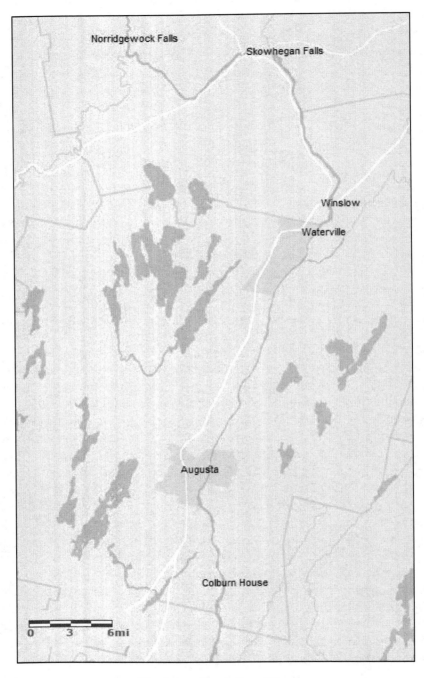

The lower Kennebec River

I was to be disappointed – it was not an expression of surprise that spread across his face but a knowing nod of his head. "So you're doing Arnold's Trail. Heard about someone doing it back in the '70's but nobody since." Perhaps he had read about Duluth or Parker and Frank – they had all received some press when they did it. "Well, good luck!"

"Do you come here often?" I asked.

"Sure. Live up the bank a ways and come here to relax. Small game trail down to the river back there." He gave an expansive wave of his hand that encompassed both banks. I looked around but could spot no trail. He certainly must have dropped from the sky, I therefore assumed, and quite likely made a not-insignificant splash while doing so.

I thanked him and continued. Later, a brief chat with a fisherman elicited a similarly knowing response. While I myself had read extensively about the trip, I had understood that to most people, Arnold's march was simply a forgotten footnote in history. Most of my friends and family had given me a blank stare when I introduced the topic to them – they had no prior knowledge. Apparently, however, Arnold's endeavors were better known in Maine than I had thought.

The paddling to Fort Halifax was fairly simple – I was forced to hop out of the boat once to drag briefly over a shallow section but otherwise was able to paddle the entire way, enjoying the wildlife and sights. It was a pretty stretch of river.

· · ·

Arnold, on the other hand, likely felt like he had no time to stop and smell the flowers. Although he had badly underestimated both the required time and distance to Quebec, he was still under no illusions that it would be a walk in the park. His orders to subordinates throughout late September include such instructions as, "hurry on as fast as possible without fatigueing the men too much," and "forward on all the provisions here as fast as possible to Fort Halifax."[2] He knew time was of the essence if he was going to beat the weather. Already, the men woke to clothing that had frozen, "a pane of glass thick" one morning and they too were feeling the press of time.[3] Winter would come sooner than desired.

Waters that I was able to easily navigate proved more challenging for Arnold and his men. A Class II rapid named Six Miles Falls gave them pause and other swift sections challenged them nearly as much. As many of the men struggled and cursed at the bateaux, others marched on the rough road that paralleled the river between Forts Western and Halifax, left over from when the two forts were active. This would be the easiest marching of the trip for the walkers.

With their still-nascent paddling abilities, the men struggled through even these straightforward rips. If they had known what awaited them, doubtless many would have quit right there. Dearborn describes the river here as "a very rapid stream"[4] and Thayer goes further, stating that "Our men are obliged to wade more than half their time."[5] But in the end they endured relatively little trouble to arrive at Fort Halifax. Any challenges faced were a mere scratching of the surface of what was to come.

Fort Halifax is placed at the junction of the Kennebec and Sebasticook Rivers on a low spit of land jutting into the river. Here, the men found "Two Large Block Houses and a Large Barrack which is inclosed by a Picquet Fort."[6] However, it was "in a ruinous state" and "did not admit of much comfort."[7] The men did not rest here long but continued to the first portage, just upstream, around Ticonic Falls.

Ticonic Falls, which according to Arnold means "good carrying place", was the first obstacle that the men faced that required a portage of their boats and equipment. As described in the above Interlude, this was accomplished in various ways but, since it was the first carry of the trip, there were no doubt some rough spots to iron out and techniques to be fine-tuned. It took each division most of a day to travel the short distance required. Some locals flocked with their carts and oxen to aid the army over the carry (for a fee of course – Yankee thrift and frugality did not become a cliché out of nothing). Here too the men paused to repair their boats, many of which were already in dire straits. Colburn and his men were in the rear and therefore could not help many of the more forward troops.

Following Ticonic Falls, a long stretch of quickwater named Five Mile Ripples (or Rapids) lay in front of the army. It was "very dangerous and difficult to pass,"[8] wrote Arnold and Dr. Senter agreed. "In these rapids the water was in general waistband high. With their united efforts, the stream was so violent as many times to drive them back after ten or twelve fruitless attempts [to advance]."[9] George Morison had similar complaints. "In pulling the bateaux through the rapids, shoals and shallows, it frequently happened that some of the men plunged over the head into the deep basons formed by the concussion of the water against the large rocks...these impediments were numerous until we arrived at the head of the river...Not once in the whole course of the passage from Fort Halifax to the head of the Kenebeck, was there an occasion for rowing."[10]

The struggle of constant wetting and immersion in the river was complicated by the weather. It continued to grow colder and the men battled freezing temps at night. They built huge fires to ward off the chill and attempt to dry their clothes, with limited success. "Last night it froze so Hard as to freeze our wet clothes that we did not Lie upon,"[11] lamented William Humphrey and many other journalists concurred. This did not stop them, however, nor appear to even slow their progress, and the army marched onwards.

· · ·

As I paddled along the Kennebec, I liked to imagine their blazing campfires on the banks of the rivers. Because the army was split into four divisions, each moving at their own speed, campsites were numerous along the river banks. Where possible, rear divisions made use of campsites created by forward detachments, but this was not always feasible. Portage take-outs and put-ins made especially good campsites since that meant one less loading/unloading of the boats.

Arnold described camping approximately four miles south of Fort Halifax and the night of my first day I decided that was a good spot to spend the evening as well. I likely missed his exact site, however, since I chose a small level area on the side of a steep hill; it was tucked in the trees near a small stream where I would bother no one. Arnold probably picked a much larger swath of smooth open ground. Burritos formed my inaugural dinner on the trail and I, well pleased with my own progress, ate hungrily while looking out over the river.

Few locations lend themselves better to reflection than the banks of a river or stream. Water flowing smoothly and steadily seems to encourage reflection, and solitude only amplifies the feeling. After finishing dinner and cleaning the pot, I could simply sit and muse, since there was literally nothing else that I needed to do. At home, there are always chores and items on the honey-do list – pay the bills, do the laundry, fix the wobbly chair, vacuum, the list goes on and on. Should one choose to put them off, they still remain there in the back of one's mind, a small nagging thought, like a splinter that won't go away.

But in the woods, those chores disappear. They are inaccessible and therefore don't exist. That first night, I pulled out my journal and wrote several pages, then tossed it aside and leaned back into the hill. I had found a spot that, with a root on one side and a lump in the ground on the other, seemed form-fitted for my rear end. A jacket bunched up made a great pillow.

And I let my thoughts wander over the events of the day, my just finished meal – what a delicious burrito, and the day to come. Then they wandered further. "What's Elizabeth doing right now?" "Boy I could really use a Boston crème donut." "I hope the Red Sox are winning." And I took in my surroundings, watching a large bug struggle to overcome a twig – clearly an obstacle to whatever bug-business it was hurriedly going about.

This was the feeling that I come out into the woods for. The outer beauty forms a perfect backdrop for the inner serenity I find when amongst the trees and animals. As I watched the creatures of the earth go about their business and observed the ever-changing environment around me, I knew that this was a feeling that I would continue to search out for the rest of my life.

I arrived at Fort Halifax mid-morning on my second day. The sun was burning brightly overhead and I grounded my canoe on a sandy beach where a sole man stood, to all appearances welcoming my arrival with a cup of coffee.

Alas, the coffee was for his own enjoyment so I walked across a green park covering the spit of land to some slightly higher ground where the only remnant of the once larger fort remains: a blockhouse.* It was a two-story square building, the second story having larger dimensions than the first which allowed defenders to be able to rain down weapons on attackers and water on fires. It still appeared solid and I walked a circle around it but besides for a brief interpretive panel there was little to see.

Ticonic Falls is now enhanced by a dam, making the change in water level more drastic but the portage shorter. I hop-scotched along the exposed bedrock on river left with the boat and gear a short hundred yards and put in above on some wooden slats that were part of the dam infrastructure.

One of the major changes in river make-up that I faced in the 21st century was the proliferation of dams. Maine has a strong history of damming rivers for navigation and power, and the Kennebec has seen its fair share. Structures flew up on many rivers throughout the first half of the twentieth century and there is nary a waterway without some obstruction. While there is a movement afoot currently to remove some of the dams, it is a costly and politically challenging process and only a few have been successfully dismantled.

Dams offered a bittersweet impediment for me. While they irrevocably changed the composition of the river, they also improved my own navigation significantly. Where Arnold struggled up Five Mile Ripples, I was able to paddle easily across the flat impoundments behind both the Waterville and Winslow dams with little trouble. What had once been a tumbling, challenging river was now a sedate pond. Given the choice, I'd take the original river, but unfortunately it was not up to me.

The river after the dam at Ticonic Falls was flanked by old mill buildings built right to the river's edge. I paddled along the base of one, peering into inky cement caverns underneath the structure, listening to the drip, drip, drip of water within and smelling the accompanying refuse of the "improved" riverbank. Yuck.

Shortly afterwards, Winslow Dam appeared around the corner. A more significant structure, it rose dozens of feet out of the river. River left (my right heading upstream) appeared blocked by cliffs so I took out on river right and scrambled up an incredibly steep bank unencumbered to a road along the top, searching for a route around. A pick-up truck pulled over immediately.

"Can I help you?" the man within asked. He wore a uniform and spoke in a tone that implied he was interested in anything but being helpful.

"Just trying to find the portage trail around the dam. Guidebook said it was on this side," I smiled in an effort to be friendly. He did not make the same

---

* It too was briefly absent – in 1987 a flood carried it downstream all the way to Augusta. It had to be trucked back to its original site and reconstructed.

attempt.

"You're trespassing and they won't hesitate to fine you," he said. He was not the type to beat around the bush, apparently. It was also clear that a fine might please him more than my appearance had, though I suspected it would not elicit a smile. He did not appear to be the smiling type.

"Who's 'they'?" I asked. After all, it would be tough to be fined if I didn't know who it was doing the deed.

"The railroad. You're on private railroad property. No trespassing. They've fined people before."

That I didn't doubt. I asked if he was aware of a portage trail in the area, knowing the answer already as the words left my mouth. He responded in the negative before repeating his threat of a fine for a third time.

Not wanting him to think I was simple, I let him know I got the message and beat a hasty retreat over the guardrail and back down the impossibly steep bank. The top of the dam ended approximately two-thirds of the way up the bank, but it would be a bear to get there. If there was any alternative, it would be better than here.

I returned to the canoe, paddled across the river and scouted the far bank. As I had seen from a distance, it was cliffy and at the very top was an impassable chain-link fence. I re-paddled across the channel back to river right and unloaded.

To get up the steep bank with the canoe on my shoulders, I made use of a length of rope tied to the top of the dam. It ended up being half-scramble and half-rappel to get up the bank. The tumpline allowed me to keep the canoe balanced without the use of my hands, though my neck ended up doing a lot of the work, and by working up hand over hand up the rope, I made it to the top of the dam (though still below the guardrail, road and the no-trespassing-or-we'll-fine-you railroad property). I walked briefly along the top of the dam, past some no-trespassing-or-we'll-fine-you signs posted by the hydropower company, to the upstream side only to find a railing topping a six-foot drop back down to the water.

I shook my head. This could not be how this dam was meant to be portaged, but I had found no other route. I loaded the canoe on top of the dam and then slid it gently under the railing (it just fit) on top of the dam until it was cantilevered out over the water with the railing holding it in place, thinking to myself, "Only a durable ABS boat would do this for me and be no worse for the wear." I jumped down into the shallow water and worked the boat above me the rest of the way through the slot and into the water. Voila! I had managed to trespass on both dam and railroad property in one portage but I had made it. Very pleased with myself I looked around for an audience. I felt like I deserved a round of applause. But no one was in sight so I climbed in and paddled on.

I quickly passed under I-95, with signs facing the water warning of bridge construction. Perhaps falling debris was an issue, though I saw none. A third dam barred my way soon after, but, much to my surprise and pleasure, a well-marked portage trail appeared on river right. It was a quick 75 meters before I was back on the water. An old man sat at the put-in on a rock looking out over the water, lost in contemplation. I let him be but as I climbed in he asked, "Where are you going?"

"Quebec," I answered.

He laughed. "Hope you get there!"

"Me too!" I airily replied, but it was true. I did hope I got there and it wasn't a sure thing yet.

. . .

Arnold, by this point, likely had similar feelings. The river was proving more challenging than anticipated and he may have even begun to suspect that the distance was not as short as his information told him. It was still with high spirits, however, that the men advanced. Despite the challenging river, cold weather, and slow advance, they were on full rations and still enjoying the adventure and hard work.

Where I portaged around dams, the men waded upstream, dragging their boats with them. "At 12 o'clock, set out again for Squhegan Falls; the stream is very swift, which makes it difficult, and our Batteaux leaky, besides the place being very shallow, which obliges our men to go into the river and haul Batteaux after them, which generally occupies three or four men, two of whom are at her head and one or two at her stern, which occasioned a slow progress," narrates Simeon Thayer, and indeed, the next large obstacle for the army was Skowhegan Falls.[12]

Thayer states that, "The carrying place is very difficult being obliged to carry our provisions and Batteaux up a steep rocky precipice,"[13] which does no justice to the difficulty of the carry. Abner Stocking perhaps describes it best when he wrote that, "We had to ascend a ragged rock, near 100 feet in height and almost perpendicular, though it seemed as though we could hardly ascend it, we succeeded in dragging our batteaus and baggage up it."[14]

Most modern-day historians are amazed at the feat for, upon close examination of the cliff face that they must have used, it appears nigh impossible to surmount. The river splits around an island here, cascading over waterfalls on each side. Supposedly an old American Indian portage trail went up and over the island, but whereas American Indians would have carried only a canoe (if that – often they would leave a boat on each side of a well-used portage to eliminate having to carry one) and minimal gear, the army followed with its monstrous bateaux and mountains of baggage. Yet there can be little doubt that surmount it they did for all journalists agree that the portage went over the island. What is most amazing is that while Stocking provides a fair description, few other journalists comment on the difficulty. We can only assume that it merely presented itself as one challenge among many to the other narrators. Arnold himself simply states that they "reached Sou Heagan Falls which we passed..."[15] After seeing it in person, one can't help suspecting that he used more curses while passing it than he used words to describe it in his journal.

The river did not relent. "Our men are as yet in very good spirits, considering they have to wade half the time , and our boats so villainously constructed, and leaking so much that they are always wet,"[16] complained Simeon Thayer, and others did not disagree. The river continued to act as one long unremitting obstacle to progress, and their hastily constructed bateaux offered no help. As the craft soaked and dried, soaked and dried, the wood warped and shrank, exposing large gaps between planks. After the Skowhegan Falls portage most boats needed serious repairs. Journals are peppered with statements like, "We ha[u]led up our Batteaus and Clear'd them for overhauling," or "we hall'd up our Batteaus and Caulk'd them, as well as we could they being very leaky,"[17] throughout this section of river as boat crews continuously knocked against rocks and the river bottom.

Yet the men found some time for contemplation and peaceful reflection as well. In the evenings, after the food was cooked and eaten, boats repaired, and gear stowed, the men were able to relax before bed. "Encamped in a most delightful wood, where I thought I could have spent some time agreeably in solitude, in contemplating the works of nature,"[18] exulted Abner Stocking near Skowhegan, and he was not alone. Dorr family tradition holds that when William Dorr camped near Augusta, ME, he thought it was so beautiful that he returned to the area after the expedition was over to settle, starting a family and helping to found the town of Hallowell, ME nearby.[19] While the men fought and struggled upstream on the Kennebec, they were still able to take in and appreciate the innate beauty of the natural world around them.

Before long, the army arrived at Norridgewock Falls, the next obstacle. It was now early October and wintry weather was in the offing, but even the resultant sense of urgency did not prevent most divisions from taking more than a day to navigate the mile-long portage around the series of short drops that make up the falls. "We saw an altar constructed by the Indians and the remains of a Roman chapel,"[20] wrote Simeon Thayer, and many others commented on the unique sight. In 1724, amidst frontier unrest, a party of colonials had moved against the American Indian village here and massacred most inhabitants, along with the resident missionary, Father Rale (perhaps not just an innocent bystander, he was accused of inciting the American Indians to depredations against the colonists). The few surviving Norridgewocks, for so the tribe was called, moved away and a few Europeans had since moved in. The remnants of the American Indian village were still visible and many men took a brief moment to examine them.

Norridgewock represented the last vestiges of civilization on the Kennebec River: from here until the first settlements in Quebec the army would find no more farms or houses. The occasional purchase of fresh fruit and vegetables from settlers in the river valley ceased north of Norridgewock and Benedict Arnold spent his final night under a roof here with a "widow Warren." Several local oxen and wagons aided the portage around Norridgewock Falls, but this too ceased further north. As Abner Stocking notes, "The remainder of our route was to be through a trackless wilderness. We now entered a doleful barren woods."[21] The army was now truly on its own.

. . .

I too was enjoying the scenery and accompanying peace, silence and solitude. While I had no immediate plans to settle in the valley myself, it certainly made for pleasant paddling. Many of the journalists commented on the lush farmland and verdant beauty of the shore, and 240 years have done nothing to change that.

I spent both my second and third nights on islands in the river, taking advantage of the seclusion they provided to avoid potential confrontation with any protective landowners. The second night I pitched my tent in the very center of a small island in a small patch of ferns, with thick bushes obscuring any view of the river on all sides. As I was eating dinner, a pair of kayakers circumnavigated the small landmass, and I was treated to a conversation including an update on the recent local town meeting. They had no idea I was there and that was fine with me.

I woke early on the morning of my third day and set off for Skowhegan Falls, only several miles upstream from my island campsite. A gorge preceded the falls proper and a low dam crossed the river just downstream from the gorge. I hauled my canoe over the cement barrier and then paddled and lined up the south shore of the gorge, jumping from tiny eddy to tiny eddy to avoid the fast-moving water in the center. The gorge was not much longer than 1000 meters and at the end I was faced with two dams on either side of a small rocky island, undoubtedly the "steep rocky precipice" of the journals.

I paddled around the base of it, from one dam to the other, before setting my paddle across the gunwales in amazement. Just how did they do it?! I shook my head in amazement. Getting a canoe up the face would be near impossible, let alone a 400-pound bateau. They must have used a series of ropes to haul the boats up the nearly vertical surface. There was simply no other way.

But I wanted to follow their portage – I had searched out all references to it in their journals the night before in my tent and was feeling excited about the challenge. So I tied my bow painter to a struggling bush perched precariously in a small crevice of the rock and scrambled to the top to try and figure out the best way up. At the top, however, I was defeated. Buildings were built across the entire top of the cliff, from dam to dam, blocking access except for one small section where an eight-foot chain link fence barred the way. I would have to find an alternative route.

I ferried across the dam outflow to river right and took out on some jumbled rocks. A sign nearby pointed to a portage route which spit me out on the road. I crossed a busy street, canoe on my shoulders, pack on my back and with horns honking in support, before putting in on the upstream side of the island in a dead water. A small plaque to Arnold's trip was set into an adjacent rock. A nearby church generously allowed me to refill my water bottles and I continued on my way.

The stream between Skowhegan and Norridgewock Falls was relatively gentle aside from some fast water that currently makes up Bombazeen Rips. Journalists again note wading and poling through the rapids here but I managed with simply some hard paddle strokes and the occasional push off the riverbed with my paddle.

As I paddled along, parts of the river seemed to become more and more like a mountain stream. Gone were the deep waters of the lower Kennebec, and gone too were the industrial-sized mill buildings built right to the river's edge. Instead I passed farmland and forests. A woman and her son threw rocks for a dog at one point – he'd bury his head in the water to retrieve them (although who knows if he managed to grab the right one every time). I startled a beaver paddling around one bend, and birds continued to swoop and soar above me. Gone too was the incessant traffic noise of the more heavily populated areas. The Kennebec was becoming more and more pleasant to paddle.

Norridgewock Falls is now dammed as well and I took a long portage to avoid the falls and accompanying hydropower infrastructure. Part of the carry was along the aptly named Arnold Road and I put in near another plaque commemorating the achievement – more proof that Mainers, at least, appreciate and memorialize the trip. I camped soon after, my third night and second on an island, and as I fell into an exhausted sleep, I listened to the sound of crickets and distant traffic. Both were soothing but it would have been nicer the way Arnold had it, with only the crickets. He left civilization, such as it was in the 18th century, at Norridgewock but clearly I was not done with it here in the 21st.

Interlude: Their Gear – What They Carried and Wore

"My wardrobe was scanty and light. It consisted of a roundabout jacket, of woollen, a pair of half-worn buckskin breeches, two pairs of wollen stockings, (bought at Newburyport,) a hat with a feather, a hunting-shirt, leggings, a pair of mockasins, and a pair of tolerably good shoes, which had been closely hoarded."[1] – John Henry

The army was carrying an immense amount of equipment and armaments. Dr. Isaac Senter made an estimate at 65 tons for the entire equipage of the trip, in addition to which he added 35 tons of food, and several historians have agreed with this estimate.[2] Over every mile of river and along every mile of portage this equipment needed to be brought along with the men. So what did it consist of? Food will be treated in the following 'Interlude' and so will not be addressed here. But that leaves 65 tons of stuff. What was it?

The boats, paddles, oars, and poles made up a large portion of that weight, perhaps 40 or more tons according to Senter. They have received adequate treatment already so let's continue down the inventory.

Each soldier's personal equipment also took up a lot of weight and space. The average soldier in Arnold's army likely had a similar wardrobe to that explained by John Henry above and "consisted of a roundabout jacket, of woollen, a pair of half-worn buckskin breeches, two pairs of wollen stockings, (bought at Newburyport,) a hat with a feather, a hunting-shirt, leggings, a pair of mockasins, and a pair of tolerably good shoes, which had been closely hoarded."

Aaron Burr also made a stab at describing his clothing when he writes a letter to his sister from Fort Western. "To begin at the Foot – over a Pr. Of Boots I draw a Pr. Of Woolen Trousers of coarse Coating. A short double breasted Jacket of the same, over this comes a Present from a Southern Gentleman – a short Shirt after the Rifle fashion – curiously fringed, with a Belt as curious. By Way of Hat another Present – A small round Hat with the Brim turn'd up – on Top a large Fox Tail with a black Feather curled up together – the Donor I suppose meant to help my Deficiency in Point of Size. My Blanket slung on my Back, as that's a thing I never trust from me. To these add a Tommahawk, Gun, Bayonet &c. and you have your Brother Aaron – And pray how do you like him?"[3]

Clothing was made of linen and wool. Few men had uniforms although each was given a frock and coat at the outset of the expedition. Their wardrobes typically consisted, as Burr and Henry described, of the shirts on their backs, the pants on their legs, perhaps a spare of either, a hat, blanket, and shoes(moccasins wore out too quickly and Henry likely had to swap his out soon after they set out). So haphazard was their clothing that officers wore a cockade to distinguish rank and when they finally attacked Quebec, the men wore a hemlock sprig in their caps to distinguish each other from the enemy.

Daniel Morgan's riflemen wore a slightly adapted outfit, as they dressed "to ape the manners of savages."[4] While this implies buckskin clothing (and Burr backs this up in his description above), many riflemen also probably used linen or wool clothing that would dry faster and not freeze as easily when wet. Blankets were used by all soldiers as an extra winter layer during the day and as bedding during the night, and were clearly a hot commodity as Burr references. And regardless of who they were, most men were forced to do as Meigs did when it rained. "I turned out and put on my clothes and lay down again and slept well till morning."[5] If they wanted dry clothes, they had to sleep in them, for few had garments to spare.

I was carrying a similar amount of clothing but due to warmer temperatures, I refused to wear wet clothes to bed. It simply made for unpleasant sleeping. Instead, I endured the unenviable routine of simply donning the sodden garments again in the morning. It inevitably invoked a shiver of displeasure down my spine and on wet mornings I fervently hoped for sun.

Guns and ammunition were another large part of the weight carried on the expedition. Muskets (typically owned by farmers who needed a cheap, durable gun) and rifles (owned by frontiersman who needed a more accurate gun for protection and hunting) were property of the individual soldiers – the Continental Army could not yet afford to issue armaments to all its members. Muskets were the preferred weapon by Washington and upper officers due to its quick firing capability, low cost of manufacture, and ability to hold a bayonet. Riflemen, however, served a vital purpose as well as a sort of light infantry although the sense of independence of the frontiersmen who made up these ranks sometimes clashed with the army's strict sense of discipline and rigid structure. Bayonets, cartridge boxes, powder, ammunition, a knife and perhaps a small hatchet or axe made up the remainder of each soldier's weaponry.

While food was basic (see the following 'Interlude'), utensils and pots were needed at the very least to cook. A group of five or six men would share a tent and cook together in a "mess". They shared the cooking utensils and a tent and likely alternated carrying them. Each man did have his own personal utensils, however, and also carried a small amount of personal gear such as razors, soap, pipe, flint and steel and maybe playing cards. Officers were permitted a little additional weight for their own personal items and may have included a few extravagances.

I carried all these basics including tent, sleeping bag and pad (luxuries over their blankets), axe and food. My own extravagances including several books and a cell phone for emergencies – luckily never needed. I carried it all on my back on portages and so like the expedition, I did not have a lot of room to spare.

Repair materials such as caulking and nails for the boats, shovels and axes for clearing portage trails and cutting firewood, and smaller items like medical supplies and instruments for the few musicians along complete the picture of the mountain of gear the army set off with. There was enough weight that the gunwales of the bateaux were not far from the river's surface, and that was even with many of the men walking along the riverside. Armies do not travel light, but Arnold was strict upon setting out that the men limit the things they bring with them, and 100 tons was about as light as the expedition could be expected to travel.

Chapter 4: The Upper Kennebec River

"You would have taken the men for amphibious animals, as they were great part of the time under water."[1] – Benedict Arnold

Above Norridgewock Falls, a series of boom piers dot the center of the river. Every four hundred feet or so a tiny island of rotting logs and jumbled rocks topped with a dusting of soil and scrub splits the river in two. These piers are a relic from the age of river logging, when logging outfits used the rivers to get timbers from the forests to the mills. By constructing a series of these piers, the loggers were able to anchor chained booms that channeled and directed the floating logs to the proper mills. No longer needed, they stand as a relic to a bygone era.

    I paddled around several of these but found little to see. They no longer had any purpose and would not suffice even to camp on because, in addition to being not much larger than the footprint of a large tent, they were thickly covered in impenetrable bushes. The last timber drives occurred in the 1970's on the Kennebec and indeed on Parker and Frank's expedition they described the river as looking like "a parquet floor" at points. Twice they had to exit the water due to the impassable pulp wood floating on the surface, an obstacle that in 2013 would not impede me. Due to more economical methods of shipping lumber combined with a heightened environmental awareness of the damage caused by these massive log drives, these picturesque log drives of yore are no more.

    Just upstream from Norridgewock Falls, the Carrabasset River enters the Kennebec. Above this confluence, the river takes on some of the characteristics of a smaller stream. Shallows, shoals, and rocks abound. I was frequently fighting Class I rips, occasionally Class II, and my pace slowed as the elevation gain increased.

. . .

    Arnold, by this point, was urging his men on ever faster, for yet another challenge was staring them in the face. As they unpacked and repacked the bateaux, and opened casks of food for consumption, they found an unhappy circumstance. Much of the food was going or had already gone bad. An

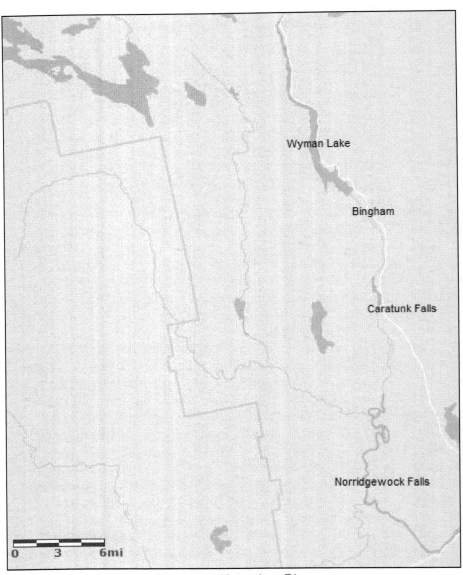

The upper Kennebec River

accounting of all edibles was in order and after checking the food, they found the "great part of which is damaged by the Boats leaking, & the difficulty of passing the Rapids, where it is impossible for People unacquainted to get up the boats without ship[ping] water."[2] "The fish," added Senter, "lying loose in the batteaux, and being continually washed with the fresh water running into the batteaux," fared poorly as well. "The bread casks not being water-proof, admitted the water in plenty, swelled the bread, burst the casks, as well as soured the whole bread. The same fate attended a number of fine casks of peas." Finally, the beef, "being killed in the heat of the summer took much damage after salting."[3] The food, however, was deemed to still be enough for everyone to remain on full rations so the army disposed of the bad, repacked, and continued upstream.

The final obstacle on the Kennebec for Arnold was Caratunk Falls, variously called "Hell Gate Falls" or "Devil's Falls" by some of the diarists. Meigs jotted down a description. "Here the river is confined between 2 rocks not more than 40 rods wide. These rocks are polished curiously in some places by the swift running water."[4] Abner Stocking simply noted that they "are of astonishing height and exhibit an awful appearance,"[5] a description that appears to work equally well. With no oxen to help them, the men were on their own but this was a short carry and they seemed to not have too much trouble navigating the trail. This was the final carry on the Kennebec River for the invading army.

· · ·

Just below present-day Caratunk Falls lies Evergreen Campground, a commercial campground with all the associated amenities. It sits, however, on the site where 240 years prior several companies from the expedition camped and even earlier an American Indian village rested. As I paddled by early on the morning of my fourth day, I paid particular attention to the spot and judged it to indeed be an excellent site to spend a night (although now that it was run as a business, I specifically avoided it. I was looking for somewhere quieter to spend my evenings.)

As I paddled past, three middle-aged women drifted towards me heading downstream in kayaks. One had a cup of coffee sitting in front of her on the deck of her boat, which she sipped occasionally as she floated.

"That coffee sure looks like a nice way to enjoy a morning paddle," I commented, being friendly. She agreed. I nodded at the other two, and paddled onwards, assuming the interaction to be over.

Moments after passing them, however, one of them hollered, "Now that sure is a good-lookin' reason to paddle back upstream!"

Unsure if she was talking to me, and unclear as to what she was saying, I tilted my head back towards them to hear better.

She let out an even louder yell, "Watch out! I'm going a cougarin'!" and then cackled the laugh of a lifetime smoker, the others chortling along with her.

I waved my hand in acknowledgement of the compliment but paddled just a little bit harder. I wanted none of what she was offering.

It was a beautiful day. I stopped on one spit of land, jutting out into the river current, and ate lunch as I watched the river drift by. Peanut butter and jelly never tasted so good. Topham related that, "the land here is low and very fine Grass, but on the edge of the river it appears to Be overflowed in the spring..."[6] and as I munched my sandwich in the shade of some trees, I noticed he was right. Flotsam was mired in the branches of the surrounding brush and trees, as high as eye-level. I took a quick tour through the area and found beach chairs, lone sandals, and construction debris hung up as well, testament to the fluctuation of the water levels through here.

Soon after lunch I paddled up to the base of Caratunk Dam. I would have loved to have seen Caratunk Falls in its natural state. Like so many other drops in Maine, the dam has blocked up this natural falls, irrevocably changing it, and the run out below has been severely rerouted by the Army Corps of Engineers, to the extent that the river no longer runs through its original bed but rather through a straightened power canal. One could still visualize the river shooting between two rocks in a powerful cataract, but it was only in the mind's eye. I portaged over a number of sharp, jagged rocks on river left before bumping into an ATV trail and putting in on the upstream side of the dam.

The river immediately south of Bingham included some of the most challenging water I had yet faced. A strong current faced me, and with few protective eddy I battled relentlessly, at times fighting hard for what felt like only inches to continue to advance. It was certainly no picnic and I felt at last that I was experiencing some of the challenge that Arnold's men had faced with their bateaux.

As I passed by the town of Bingham, I met two kids, perhaps 8 and 6 years old, fishing. I nodded but didn't speak, knowing the shyness of kids at that age.

"Well it sure is a nice day to be doing this," announced the older of the two. I was so surprised I couldn't respond with anything but a word of agreement. His voice had the tone of a delivered script line and If he had added a "Mister" to the end of it, he could have been auditioning for a 1950's sit-com. His sister, playing nearby, announced, "I'm swimming," to which I cordially agreed as well. Their mother would have been so proud had she heard – at such a young age capable of passing polite pleasantries with a stranger.

My fourth night I camped below Wyman Dam, on yet another island, among some brambles. Arnold commented here that "we encamped late at night much exhausted"[7] and I had similar sentiments, taking a quick nap before dinner. Afterwards, however, I stepped out of the bushes onto the shore and took some time to watch the sun set over the nearby mountains.

As a young boy, I had pored over maps of northern Maine, trying to find spot the most remote territory I could and then would imagine building a house at such a location. I would fish and garden for food, I'd pictured, and read books by firelight in the evenings. It had seemed to my young mind as the epitome of bliss – that small cabin in the middle of nowhere in Maine – and those dreams of solitary log cabins had kept me enthralled for what seemed like hours at a time. Standing now on the shores of the Kennebec, I was situated in such a way as to be able to see no roads, power lines, or other signs of human impact. It brought a smile to my face. If my eight year-old self could have seen me now, he would have been ecstatic.

But it was something else that elicited a rueful shake of my head. As I stood on the shore, I noticed an odd circumstance. The water appeared to be much lower than when I had pulled my boat out of it to camp, only two short hours prior. I double-checked and sure enough, the stream was running gentler and lower. Camped just below Wyman Dam as I was, to get here I had been paddling against a dam release all afternoon: a periodic increase in the amount of water that a dam operator allows to pass through the dam gates. If only I had been paddling now in the evening, I would have had a much easier time of it! You can't win them all.

. . .

Above Caratunk Falls, the expedition encountered an even shallower and more convoluted stream. "Here the mountains begin to appear on each side the river, high, & snow on the tops and appear well wooded – the river from Norridgewalk to the G[reat] Carrying Place is very uneven in width, but in general about 400 yards & full of a great number of small islands..."[8] They were paddling through some very pretty country, but couldn't take much time to enjoy it.

They were nearing the end of their time on the Kennebec River. The Kennebec continues to head due north towards its source at Moosehead Lake. The easiest way into Canada, however, is via the Dead River, a tributary of the Kennebec that flows from the west. By following the Dead River, they would come to a relatively low height of land, a portage over which would place them in the Chaudière River watershed and well on their way to Quebec.

Just before the Dead meets the Kennebec, it turns a wide arc northwards while simultaneously dropping steeply in elevation. In order to avoid this, American Indians for generations had portaged through a series of ponds (today aptly named West, Middle, and East Carry Ponds) to eliminate both the extra miles and heavy whitewater. This series of portages continues to be known by same the name which Arnold knew it as: the Great Carrying Place (today placed squarely in the Carrying Place Township).

In his journal, Montresor noted only that, "a little above the portage a remarkable brook falls into the [Kennebec], which forms the first or nearest lake,"[9] by way of route-finding description. Arnold appears to have had little trouble finding the start of the portages himself and noted in more detail: "When abreast of the Carrying Place in the River, you will observe at ab[out] 400 yards above you a large mountain in shape of a shugar Loaf – at the foot of which the River turns off to the Eastward – This Mountain when you are at the carrying Place seems to rise out of the middle of the river…"[10] With such a detailed description, it would be tough to miss and the "shugar Loaf" is today known as Henhawk Ledge. On October 10th, 1775, it came into the view of the vanguard of the army. They had reached the Great Carrying Place and conquered the Kennebec. But their journey was just beginning.

．　．　．

I was not able to experience the final meanderings of the Kennebec the way Arnold did. Wyman Dam, the most impressive of the Kennebec River barriers, stands 155 feet tall just north of Bingham, Maine. The impoundment behind it is Wyman Lake, one of the larger lakes in Maine. Paddling up to it, the structure simply gets larger, and larger, and larger. I canoed nearly to the base, avoiding the outflow, and simply sat and stared up at the edifice for a while before looking for the portage. It was certainly the largest dam I had ever been that close to.

River right was forested so I took out river left which was wide open and had a passable track leading from river's edge up and over the heavily altered and tiered embankment.

Once at the top of the bank, however, I knew I was on the wrong side. Thousands of yards of open space stared at me, dotted with power line towers. A spider web of lines creased the sky in front of me and a chain-link fence topped with barbed-wire barred my way to the lake's edge for as far as I could see. I knew I didn't want to portage through that – if nothing else, walking under all those power lines would likely fry my brain.

Looking back across the river to river right, I found what I hadn't seen before: a gravel landing tucked behind a large boulder. That felt right. So I reloaded and crossed the river to the other side. Beginning to portage up the gravel road, I soon passed a sign facing the other direction. I turned around, canoe still on my shoulders, to read it, expecting a "Canoe Portage" sign. Instead, it was of course a "No Trespassing" sign. Not again!

I grinned, then shook my head, and ignored it (I was after all, moving from 'Trespassing' status to 'Not Trespassing' status by walking past it. In other words I had gone from not knowing I was trespassing to knowing that I was not trespassing). As I continued up the road, I now knew that this was not the portage, and that likely there was none marked.

Sure enough, the road led directly away from the river and presumably was used as a work road. It was certainly not meant for portaging. But I did notice a small trail, perhaps animal, that threaded between two additional "Danger: No Trespassing" signs. I decided to follow it – it seemed to head in the desired direction. I chuckled to myself as I threaded between the signs - they'll probably include 'serial trespasser' in my obituary. The trail soon petered out to nothing, but with the river on my right, I knew I was headed in the correct direction.

With a one hundred and fifty foot dam to circumvent, I knew I had some elevation to gain and sure enough, between ducking trees and scaling a steep hillside, I was forced to my knees on several occasions to make progress. The footing was too precarious and downed leaves too slippery to do otherwise in many places. If it had been 5 o'clock, I would have been frustrated, but challenges like these early in the day only get me excited. I like a good portage with my coffee in the morning.

The put-in I found was a steep, cliffy outcropping of granite which I balanced the canoe against, using a jutting cedar to help slide it into the water. It was a test of my balancing abilities to enter the boat, but I made it without mishap and was successfully on Wyman Lake. Phew!

Wyman Lake, on a beautiful sunny day such as I had, was a stunning body of water. Stretching north-south, it nevertheless has numerous inlets and coves which I paddled past. Despite knowing that this was a man-made lake, the creation of which destroyed a likely still more beautiful river, I couldn't help but enjoy myself, even taking a brief moment to lie back and absorb some sun rays.

I found the beginning of the Great Carrying Place as easily as Arnold had done. It was tucked into a corner of the lake, just where the Kennebec once again assumes its riverine form. A woods road led right down to and met me at the water's edge, and an old wooden structure – perhaps a dock section – marked the beginning of the portage. The trail was even marked with orange paint: at last, a portage trail that didn't require trespassing!

A breather was in store before I set out on the first and longest of the Great Carrying Place portages. I watched the hemlock shadows play over the water's surface and swatted bugs for a minute, pumping myself up for the three plus miles to East Carry Pond. But the portage was not going to walk itself so I loaded up my gear, threw the canoe on my shoulders, and set off. The next stage of the trip had begun.

Interlude: What Did They Eat?

"I shot a small bird called a sedee [likely a chickadee] and a squirrel which I lived upon this day."[1] – James Melvin

The proverb, "An army marches on its stomach" is often attributed to Napoleon Bonaparte. He was only six years old at the time of Arnold's march, but the adage would have rang all too true for the men as they continued their struggle northwards through Maine.

The vast quantities of food – remember Senter estimated the weight at 35 tons at the expedition's embarkation – needed to sustain the army over the long march is all the more unimaginable when one considers that every barrel needed to be toted time and time again by the men over long, rugged portages, and loaded into and unloaded from the bateaux countless times. Traditional military transports such as wagons and oxen simply didn't work and weren't feasible in the wilderness for this army. Once past Norridgewock and its helpful inhabitants, the army was on its own.

Toiling day in and day out took immense amounts of energy, which in turn required massive amounts of sustenance. A standard ration for soldiers in the Continental Army included meat, bread or flour, milk, beer or cider, molasses, vegetables, and rice or cornmeal all in large quantities. Of course, this standard ration was on paper only. Quartermasters frequently were forced to make do with what was available (milk rarely was, for example). A similar diet could be expected by Arnold's men. For example, as part of the preparations Arnold ordered Colburn to procure "five hundred Bushells of Indian Corn, all the pork and flour you can from the inhabitants…sixty barrells of salted beef of 220lbs each Barrell."[2] By the time they set out, it can be expected that full rations were available for each of the men for the expected duration of the trip. Indeed, early journal entries are peppered with references to salted beef, pork and cod, biscuits and flour, and peas.

Of course also vital to any army in the 18th century were both tobacco and liquor. The men each carried their own tobacco, and some quickly ran out. As Henry tells us, however, "In the wilderness, where the army soon run out the article of tobacco, the men had many valuable succedaneums. The barks of the different kinds of firs, the cedar, the red willow, and the leaves of many astringent or bitter plants supplied the place."[3] And liquor, at least in small amounts, was available to the men in the beginning. "As usual took our Bottle to make a drink of grog but found good creater gone which occasioned dull looks,"[4] bewailed Moses Kimball, and the army ran out fairly soon into the expedition. Henry wrote that he drank the last of the expedition's liquor at the Great Carrying Place.

This basic diet, however, was supplemented in various ways. While still among riverside farms and settlements, men would frequently purchase fresh fruits and vegetables to supplement their meals. Senter tells of making "a most luxurious supper, having received a few potatoes and carrots which I procured..."[5] One soldier even managed to find some delicacies, beginning many daily journal entries with, "This morning arose well and got some chocolate and herrings."[6] Where a common soldier found all that chocolate remains a mystery.

Hunting parties were also dispatched to supplement the stores with fresh meat. In particular the men found moose, which many called "moose deer", to be especially interesting and tasty, many having never seen one before. "We can hardly walk 50 yards without meeting their tracks; their meat is good and refreshing,"[7] notes one soldier, a sentiment shared by woodsmen of the 21st century as well. Shooting one, however, was another matter. "It is seldom they can be shot, being so swift that they disappear in an instant among the thickets and swamps."[8] One suspects that the marching army provided ample warning to any moose in the area that they had better be wary. No matter, by the time they had reached the Great Carrying Place they had bagged four and would manage a couple others in the following days.

Fishing was also a highly successful endeavor for fortifying their rations. Many of the journalists rejoiced at the amount and size of fish caught along the Kennebec and Dead Rivers, one noting that they were of "extraordinary appearance, long broad, and thick. The skin was of a very dark hue, beautifully sprinkled with deep crimson spots."[9] And in the great tradition of fish tales everywhere, Arnold brags that at one pond, "our People caught a prodigious number of fine Salmon Trout, nothing being more common than a man's taking 8 or 10 Doz in one hours time, which generally weigh half a pound a piece."[10] As historian Kenneth Roberts points out, this means that one man was catching a sizeable fish every thirty seconds for an hour straight, which of course is likely at least a slight exaggeration. In spite of all this, fishing was often a luxury since the time required for success had to be balanced with the need to make progress.

Officers had an additional way of supplementing their meals. While enlisted soldiers had strict weight limits on the amount of personal gear they were entitled to carry, officers had a little more leeway. They brought small luxuries with them including sugar, tea, coffee, butter, and other small items to complement their barreled rations. Arnold included jams, wine, and pickles amongst his own personal gear – one of the benefits of rank.

Each evening in camp men would cook their rations in messes – groups of five or six men who ate and cooked together. One would draw the rations for the group from the quartermaster and they would either rotate cooking duties or appoint one with a particular aptitude for the job, perhaps giving him a little extra for his trouble. Most 18th century armies had camp followers – frequently wives or mistresses of the men – who would sometimes help with this and other chores such as laundry and mending. Arnold's army had only four women that posterity knows about so it largely fell to the men to perform these labors as well.

Each mess had a cooking pot – a heavy cast iron pot within which all meals were cooked. It was a particularly awkward and cumbersome contrivance and the men would sometimes go to great lengths to avoid carrying and portaging the item. Meat was frequently roasted on bayonets, spits, or knives, flour was usually formed into cakes and "baked" over the fire, and cornmeal and rice went into the pot, perhaps with some pork or a little salt for flavoring. In all it was a fairly bland and unvaried but quite filling repast the men had each mealtime, when rations were plentiful.

Rations, however, were quickly dwindling. Due to a combination of factors including the leaky bateaux, poorly packed or constructed barrels, and inexperienced boatmen, the men were put on limited rations at the end of the Great Carrying Place, consisting of only ¾ pound of pork and a pint of flour per man. The beef, peas, salted fish and other food items were either exhausted or rotten beyond redemption. The last live ox, driven all the way to the end of the Great Carrying Place, was slaughtered and each man given a share, an event celebrated (likely with a touch of foreboding) by many journalists.

As supplies dwindled – rations would be reduced throughout the length of the Dead River until just past the Height of Land where all remaining rations were handed out, consisting of just a few ounces of pork and flour each – the men were forced to become more creative in their foraging. They emptied out every last bit of flour to make cakes with, and became less discerning in their hunting. Henry ate beaver tails, stating only that "Taste, however, is arbitrary, and often the child of necessity,"[11] regarding the flavor. James Melvin ate a chickadee and a squirrel one day and others nabbed rabbits, woodcocks, hawks, partridges, and even a ferret. John Henry "discovered and ate a delicious species of cranberry, entirely new to us...as large as a May-duke cherry,"[12] and likely should have counted himself lucky that he didn't become sick from eating the strange berries.*

They also discovered that moose was perhaps not all that they had

---

* In yet another uncanny parallel between Arnold's trip and Parker and Frank's journey 200 years later, near where Henry munched on his cranberries, Frank and Parker described to me a field of blueberries and ensuing feast under a shining sun after having endured several days of downpours.

originally thought it to be. "Though we gorged the stomach, the appetite was unsatisfied," complained Henry. Without the accompanying fats and oils from their pork and beef, moose on its own did not provide enough nourishment. "By this time the fat and marrow of the [moose] we had killed, were exhausted, and our stock of salt had been long since expended. One who has never been deprived of bread and salt, nor known the absence of oleaginous substances in his food, cannot make a true estimate of the invaluable benefits of such ingredients, in the sustenation of the bodily frame; nor the extremity of our corporeal debility...Though we might have killed more [moose] deer, the vigor of our bodies was so reduced that we were convinced that that kind of food could not restore us to our wonted energy..."[13] The meat was too lean to exist upon alone and in spite of eating all they could hold, it would not prevent starvation.

As their situation became ever direr, one reading their journals can almost come to the conclusion that the men made a kind of morbid game out of eating odder and odder items in an attempt to stave of hunger. The details appear in a later 'Interlude' as the crisis comes to a point but as pork, beef and flour disappeared from their diets, the men looked to bones, candles, leather from clothing or shot pouches, and even camp dogs for sustenance. It was a far cry from the envisioned daily ration including milk, molasses and spruce beer ordered by Congress.

Chapter 5: The Great Carrying Place

"Every step we made sunk us knee-deep in a bed of wet turf. My feet were pained and lacerated by the snags of the dead pines, a foot and more below the surface of the moss."[1] – John Joseph Henry

Portaging requires a certain mindset. To be able to simply allow your brain to drift and wander over myriad topics while your feet move you forward is a valuable skill, permitting you to ignore the pain and fatigue of your back, neck and shoulders.

As I took the first steps of the first Great Carrying Place portage, I knew it would be a long one – nearly three miles to the first pond. I followed a woods road, blazed orange, up a hill and soon arrived at a gravel road where a sign stood, labeling this as part of Arnold's historic route. I followed the road a ways, keeping an eye out to my left. I knew that the portage trail continued off that way soon, but was not sure where. It was a beautiful and hot day and the canoe on my shoulders acted as a bit of a sun shade. It didn't stop me from sweating profusely.

I spotted a small trail soon, but it was fainter than I expected. I set my gear down and scouted up it unburdened. It ascended steeply up a hill parallel to a stream and I satisfied myself that it was probably used as a swimming access for the mountain stream. It certainly wasn't the portage I was looking for.

Back to my gear and up the road a bit further, I easily spotted another white sign marking the route. It directed me left off the gravel and onto a woods road where I gently ascended for nearly two miles.

The trail was clearly old, although it likely had been used in the not too distant past as a logging road. Branches now loomed over the route and fallen trees occasionally blocked the way. Large ruts and gullies completed the picture and it was clear that this would not be used by motorized vehicles again anytime soon.

It was pleasant at first, walking along a fairly clear trail with branches and trunks arching overhead as a sort of natural covered walkway. But as time passed, my breath came in shorter gasps and the lactic acid began to build up in my quads and calves. I refused to slow down, however, and tried to continue to

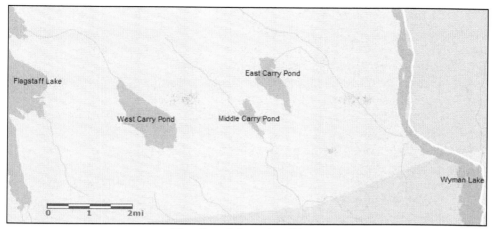
The Great Carrying Place

maintain my steady pace even in the face of steeper and more uneven terrain. I blinked quickly to try and keep the perspiration out of my eyes and re-adjusted my tump occasionally to change the location of the pressure on my head and angle of force on my neck. A tumpline makes portaging easier, but not easy – it's still incredibly hard work walking with such a burden.

    I kept thinking I was almost there, and the trail kept going up. I had trouble maintaining a good pace moving up the grade but I kept pushing. Once I arrived at the top of the hill, however, I set the canoe down and took a break – not something I like to do mid-portage but here I needed it. The sustained uphill grade did me in.

    After the insular world beneath the canoe where my own heavy breathing, the buzz of black flies, and the pain in my shoulders and neck seemed to make up my entire existence, it can be a magical thing to return to the larger world. When the weight is removed and the sounds from the surrounding forests re-enter the conscience, it instills just a mild sense of wonder, and I reveled in the water break. Suddenly just carrying my own weight felt like paradise.

    Experiencing this portage with my own lightweight gear and canoe made it all the more remarkable that Arnold's men toiled with 400-pound bateaux and 200-pound casks up it. Senter complained that "The land was almost an endless ascent from lake to lake,"[2] and he wasn't far off. I tried to picture them, watching their ghosts pass me as they dragged and carried their gear. It was nearly impossible to imagine. The strength, endurance, fortitude, and sheer stubbornness that must have inhabited these soldiers to successfully make this passage was simply overwhelmingly incomprehensible. I couldn't help but think that it was a bygone mindset, not to be found in the present day.

A red squirrel continued to interrupt my mid-portage reverie, chattering at me from a nearby fallen trunk. Though I couldn't understand his language, his tone alone told me that he was disappointed in my break. "Get your sorry butt up and moving, you lazy, no-good excuse for a canoeist," he seemed to say so I wearily loaded up and continued downhill. I wasn't going to let a squirrel shame me.

A short jaunt downhill brought me to another gravel road where a sign appeared to mark the start of the trail. But I wasn't on the first lake – East Carry Pond – yet, so without a trail to follow I cut past a "Trespassers will be shot. Survivors will be shot again." sign and walked through a group of sporting camps to put in on their waterfront. The place was desolate and no one bothered me.

I paddled across the pond – no more than a couple hundred feet width at the southern narrow end – and took out next to another sign at the start of the second portage where, it being about noontime, I stopped and ate lunch near a site of particular importance to the expedition.

. . .

The scouting party of which John Henry was a member was the first of Arnold's expedition to arrive at the Great Carrying Place. Here they "found a path tolerably distinct, which we made more so by marking trees and snagging the bushes with our tomahawks."[3]

John Montresor, the British military engineer, had been through here on his mapping expedition in 1761 and, "in order, therefore, to make these portages more remarkable, we took care to blais [blaze] all the portages from the Kennebec to lake Megantic in such a manner, as to make the way much less difficult for whoever may follow us."[4] It had been used for hundreds of years before him by American Indians as an easy bypass to circumvent a large northern loop in the Dead River just before where it enters the Kennebec which was made up of almost continuous heavy whitewater. Montresor sometimes had trouble finding the route, however, because "no nation having been more jealous of their country than the Abenaquis, they have made it a constant rule to leave the fewest vestiges of their route."[5] He and his party marked it well, however, so John Henry and the scouting party were therefore simply improving a trail that had been used and blazed before them.*

Daniel Morgan followed, arriving at the first portage on October 6th with his riflemen and immediately began clearing and improving the trail from a

---

*Montresor noted the first portage as eight miles long and although it certainly felt longer to me than the three miles it truly was, he must have severely overestimated or gotten quite lost to enable eight to be even close to correct.

narrow American Indian path to a trail at least eight feet in width – what would have been the required width to permit bateaux, men and gear to travel in both directions. The rest of the army followed and soon the woods resounded with chopping, clearing, grunting and cursing as the men portaged and cleared.

Hoisting bateaux to shoulders and either stringing food along poles or carrying it within casks, the immense luggage of the expedition slowly made its way across the first portage, some men making as many as seven or eight trips to clear the first carry. While Morgan and others made every effort to clear and improve the trail, inevitably roots, rocks and uneven surfaces tripped the men and complicated efforts at crossing. Food casks and bateaux no doubt suffered additional damage as the men staggered against rocks and trees, damage that they could ill afford since food was fast disappearing and the bateaux were quickly becoming floating wrecks.

George Morison described the portage. "This morning we hauled our batteaux from the river and carries thro' brush and mire, over hills and swamps (for we had not even the shape of a road but as we forced it) to a pond (lake)…This transportation occupied us three whole days." Echoing similar sentiments as myself, he wrote that "this was by far the most fatiguing movement that had yet befel us."[6]

Weather was no help. Rain commenced as the men continued portaging, a half mile from the first pond to Middle Carry Pond and then another two miles to West Carry Pond. It continued raining for several days straight, Ephraim Squier noting that, "It is very rainy and and we (have) no shelter but the Heavens."[7] The rain, of course, did nothing to help the portaging and Squier, a few days later, again notes conditions on the trails after the downpours. "[We] are obliged to carry over our Battooes and Barrells, the way muddy and slippery, hard for poor soldiers that have to work hard in the rains and cold, and to wade a mile and a half knee-deep in water and mud, cold enough, and after night to camp in the rain without any shelter."[8] One picturing the toiling men, lurching and struggling under their burdens and covered in dirt and mud, can't help but be awed by their endurance.

The struggle and weather did begin to take a toll on their health, however. As temperatures dropped and the rains poured down, cases of dysentery and other disease increased, so much so that a small hospital was built to hold any too sick to travel. Poor water quality in the second pond only exacerbated the situation, Senter noting that, "Many of us were now in a sad plight with the diarrhea. Our water was of the worst quality. The lake was low, surrounded with mountains, situate[d] in a morass. Water was quite yellow…No sooner had it got down than it was puked up by many of the poor fellows."[9] A final patient for the hospital was a man who chose a poor location for his evening fire – the dead tree against which he built his evening fire fell in the night and fatally injured him. Named either Arnold Hospital or Fort Meigs by the men (depending on whose journal one reads), the structure was sited quite near where I was munching lunch. Relics from it have since been found by members of the Arnold Expedition Historical Society (AEHS) and its location accurately sited on the northwest shore of Middle Carry Pond. Dr. Senter was kept busy there caring for the ailing men, and a bateau was left on each of the three Carry Ponds to ferry any sick men to the rude shelter.

In spite of the struggles, Arnold was able to report to Washington in a letter from the portages that the men "have in general acted with the greatest spirit and industry"[10] and indeed they had. It had been a struggle but the army had surmounted the Kennebec River and was now moving forward, slowly but surely, and with good morale, through this next challenge.

.   .   .

I scouted around as I snacked on peanut butter and jelly, but spotted no obvious remnants from Arnold's Hospital. Later conversations with Duluth informed me that the site was a little to the north of where I now stood. Spoons, buttons, nails, and other metal miscellany have been found there and are now on display in a small museum in Stratton, ME, where I was soon headed.

The second portage was much smoother than the first. Nearly flat and only half a mile, I fairly flew through it. Almost before I knew it, I came around the corner and there was Middle Carry Pond. A small, bright red and freshly painted cabin stood nearby, topped by a small sign which informed me it was owned by AEHS.

In spite of the quick second portage, I took stock of my situation and body and decided that that had been enough for one day. It was only 2:30 but I had portaged nearly 4 ½ miles and I was tuckered out. I assumed AEHS wouldn't mind me setting up a tent on the cabin grounds – nobody was home and I certainly wasn't going to throw a party or disturb anyone.

It was an incredibly peaceful afternoon. The site was far enough removed from all human activity that no sound of roads, cars, construction, or other machinery disturbed the stillness. The sky was clear and the temperatures just right. Two loons frolicked in the water as I watched, looking like they were having so much fun that I soon joined them for a bath myself – sorely needed.

Clouds began to move in as I cooked dinner in the handy fire pit nearby. Camped on Middle Carry Pond as I was, I was slightly nervous about using the water that so many of Arnold's men got sick off of, but it seemed to have no ill effects on me. The succeeding centuries have apparently improved its quality – something that likely few other water bodies can claim. I also looked for the fish that many of the men claimed swarmed these ponds but saw no more than normal.

I woke the next morning rested and refreshed, and paddled across the pond's short width to a small stream. The previous evening's clouds indeed brought rain but it cleared soon after I began paddling. Winding through mossy islands brought me to a small bridge where I took out. A white blaze nearby informed me I was now on the eminent Appalachian Trail. Known as the AT, it runs from Georgia to Maine and here closely follows the portage route between Middle and West Carry Ponds, touching as it does on both shores and taking a direct route between the two. I would use this trail to travel to the next pond.

I had been looking forward gleefully for several days now to a meeting with some hikers as I portaged along the AT. I myself had hiked the length of it in 2008, and I would have been floored to find someone with a canoe on their shoulders in the woods of Maine. As I loaded up and began to portage, I could just picture the unsuspecting hikers' jaws dropping as I came into sight.

Sure enough, I was not disappointed. Two-thirds of the way into the hike I met two hikers. Ready with a clever quip in answer to their flabbergasted questions, I was disappointed to find that they were both from nearby.

"You fishing the Carry Ponds?" one asked. Just my luck to have run into someone local enough to know the geography! They didn't even act surprised, let alone dumbfounded. So much for the surprise!

"Nope. Making my way to Quebec." I answered, keeping my snide opinions of today's fisherman to myself. I wanted to say that if I was a fisherman, I surely wouldn't have been caught dead portaging two miles over a hill to get to another pond but instead would have been squarely on my butt in a boat, drinking beer and walking nowhere. I instead wisely remained civil.

"Like Benedict Arnold?" he queried. Yet another well-informed Mainer! It continued to surprise me that so many knew about his trip – it appeared to have minor celebrity status throughout the state.* We chatted for a while longer before I continued on.

The put-in for this portage is right next to modern-day Arnold Point, near where parts of the army camped. The trail Arnold described as "extremely bad, being choked up with roots which we could not clear away, it being a work of time,"[11] and the trail remains so today although hikers on the AT don't mind.

Clouds continued to flit across the sky, darkening the day, but the rain did not recommence as I made my way through chop and waves across the largest of the three ponds to the final portage. This would take me to Flagstaff Lake, created in 1950 by the damming up of part of the Dead River. Arnold in

---

* Not all Mainers, however, have always been as well informed. Historian Justin H. Smith tells an amusing anecdote culled from his on-the-ground research about a conversation with a farmer near the beginning of the Great Carrying Place. A farmer, when asked if any relics from Arnold existed nearby, replied, "Oh yes, there used to be a big rock in my mowing field, with 'B.D.A. 1775' on it; but the durned thing was in the way , and I blasted it out." Smith asked, "What did those letters mean, - 'B.D.A.'?" and the farmer responded, "Why, Bennie Dick Arnold, of course.": Smith, *Arnold's March*, p. 115

1775 had to portage a significantly longer distance to reach the Dead River proper (actually putting in briefly on Bog Brook which quickly led to the Dead) but I would continue my trip on wide open Flagstaff Lake.

This was not the only advantage I enjoyed for the final portage between ponds. Where the first three had been trails, likely in similar condition to the ones that Arnold used (although already cut for me where Arnold's army had to cut them for themselves), this one was along a dirt road. It again closely followed Arnold's route but with a nice grade and solid footing I moved right along the two miles it took to get to Flagstaff Lake. Only the final third of a mile was on a trail, giving me just a taste of what Arnold faced.

I started along the gravel and a car soon drove up. It stopped nearby, its driver wanting to chat, and he inched forward as I continued to walk.

"You doing Arnold's Trail?" he asked

"Yes indeed," I grinned. "Is this the right road that'll take me to Flagstaff?" A confusing set of road signs near the beginning had put me in some doubt as to the correct direction.

"Yup. Take this road to the end, turn right on the main road for a couple hundred yards, and then left on a 4 x 4 track to the water."

"Thanks!" I waved goodbye, thankful for the added directions that would end up saving me a fair amount of trouble – I didn't know about the turn onto the main road and would certainly have gotten confused for a time had I not been informed.

Towards the middle of the carry, another truck slowed, then passed me. Moments later it came back, driving the other way, and stopped.

"Are you okay?" He looked concerned for not only my physical but also mental well-being. Finally, someone who didn't know what I was doing!

"I've got a couple of screws loose, I think, but yeah, I'm okay!" I smiled and tried to look my sanest – something not altogether entirely possible with a canoe on my head more than a mile from the nearest navigable water.

He wore a dubious expression, but nodded acknowledgement and then drove away slowly. I could see him shaking his head in confusion as he disappeared around the corner and I celebrated inwardly at finally confounding someone.

The put-in on Flagstaff was on a small bay near the southeast corner of the lake and I stretched my shoulders and neck on the shore. It was good to be through the portages and back on open water.

. . .

The Great Carrying Place threw one last obstacle in the expedition's way before it was finished with them. Where I was able to travel mostly on a road for my final portage, Arnold's men faced a very different prospect. The end of the final portage was described as a "Savanna" to the eye, but walking through it was different matter entirely. "The last mile a Spruce Swamp Knee Deep in mire all the way," tells Dearborn.[12] Submerged roots and branches tore at the men's feet and clothing, and awkward footing no doubt twisted ankles and felled men as well. "To make it much worse there was ice on top which broke through," adds John Topham.[13] Clearly the weather remained a constant enemy.

Near here John Henry and the scouting party under Lieutenant Steele returned from its foray to the Height of Land. They were a sight to behold, Henry describing the group's appearance upon arrival. "Our wan and haggard faces and meagre bodies and the monstrous beards of my companions [Henry at sixteen was likely too young to be included among the wearers of "monstrous beards" himself] …seemed to strike a deep sorrow into the hearts of the pioneers,"[14] he remembered, but some food quickly revived their bodies and minds. The news they brought soon cheered the army however – the Dead River was a wide placid river for much of its length and no hostile British or American Indians had appeared.

News was not as good from the quartermaster. An inventory of available food showed that supplies were fast diminishing and steps needed to be taken. Some of the lead divisions were carrying now only several days' worth of food, and orders were sent back to Enos' fourth division to forward up additional provisions. Major Bigelow was dispatched to Enos to "bring up as much provisions as you can spare…in particular of flour."[15] All men were put on a reduced ration of a pint of flour and ¾ pound of salt pork per day. Perhaps worse news for some, the expedition was out of liquor. Henry may have drank "the last spirits in the army"[16] upon his return with the scouts, given him by a friendly officer upon seeing their decrepit appearance. Arnold also gave orders for "a Party at the E[ast] side of the first portage [of the Great Carrying Place] to build a small Logg House for men & provisions."[17] This cabin would be a stockpile of some emergency supplies in case of retreat – something Arnold no doubt would consider under only dire circumstances.

Steele was soon in good enough shape to be sent back out on another scouting mission to begin to clear the portages leading up to the Height of Land. Arnold also dispatched two American Indians, Eneas and Sabatis along with soldiers Jaquin and John Hall, the latter a British deserter turned Continental soldier, to Quebec to gain any intelligence possible. With them, they carried a letter from Arnold. Addressed to an old business contact of Arnold's from his merchant days, it requested that the acquaintance "write me by [Eneas] of the disposition of the Canadians, the number of troops in Quebec, by whom commanded…the situation of matters in general…and in short what we have to expect."[18] Essential as this information would be, it was nonetheless a great risk to send the missive, and time would show that his trust was misplaced in at least one of the participants of this group.

The expedition at last made the aptly named Bog Brook which drained the morass they had just waded through. Described as a dozen feet across and "much deeper than wide"[19], Bog Brook was a short, easy break from both the portaging and the swiftly flowing Kennebec. They floated down it to the Dead River before continuing upstream towards Quebec. Many felt that the toughest part of the trip was over, and that Quebec would soon loom on the horizon. But the Dead would bring its own set of hazards and obstacles, and the Maine wilderness was not finished with the expedition yet.

. . .

I was sending out my own queries for advance information but they were of much less consequence than Arnold's forays. I found cell phone service on the shore of Flagstaff Lake and made two calls, one to my friend John with whom I hoped to spend that evening in Stratton on the other side of Flagstaff, and another to Duluth Wing who I hoped to meet the following morning. Duluth had led many of the relic-hunting expeditions along Arnold's route and had found numerous artifacts along the portage trails and camp sites of the army. He had also replicated the route himself in the early 1970's and I hoped to pick his brain for any useful information regarding navigation as well. Both were excited to see me, and I loaded up and dipped my paddle into the waters of Flagstaff Lake, ready to cross the water of Maine's fifth largest water body.

Interlude: In Sickness and In Health

"This Night I was Seized with a Violent Head-Ach and fever, Charles gather'd me some herbs in the woods and made me Tea of them. I drank very Hearty of it and next morning felt much Better"[1] – Henry Dearborn

As was just noted in the narrative, by this point in the expedition the poor weather and burgeoning fatigue of the men necessitated a hospital being built to house the worst of the sick. Yet for all the inclemency and exhaustion, Arnold's army had a surprising dearth of poor health. Where typical 18th century armies often faced high rates of dysentery, smallpox, and other diseases causing higher fatality rates than any military confrontation, the expedition remained in comparatively excellent health. So surprising was this fact that nearly two months since leaving Cambridge, Dr. Senter was able to marvel that a drowning incident was *"the first man drowned in all the dangers we were exposed to, and the third [lost] by casualties."*[2] So to what did the army owe its excellent health?

When Henry, looking back on the expedition years later, commented that *"it does not now occur to me that any of us were assailed by sickness during this arduous expedition,"*[3] he was exaggerating. Even upon arrival on the Kennebec and disembarkation from the sailing ships at Fort Western, Dr. Senter noted that, *"at this time several of our army were much troubled with the dysentery, diarrhea, &c."*[4] Throughout the journey up the Kennebec, various cases of dysentery cropped up, and by the time of the portages over the Great Carrying Place poor water amplified the sick cases enough to warrant the construction of "Arnold's Hospital". One case in particular elicited the sympathy and pity of several of the journalists. A Dr. Irvin (physician only in civilian life, he was an ensign in the army) *"never paid any medical attention"* to the dysentery he contracted on the Kennebec. *"When he came wading in the water every day, then lodging on the ground at night, it kept him in a most violent rheumatism I ever saw, not being able to help himself any more than a new born infant, every joint in his extremities inflexible and swelled to an enormous size."*[5] He was left at the hospital and eventually returned back downstream towards civilization, still refusing medication from Dr. Senter.

Nor was it the still rudimentary medical treatments that were then in vogue that kept disease at arm's length for most of the soldiers. These methods often included bleeding the patient, therefore of course unintentionally harming their already struggling immune system still further. Even scurvy was not completely understood. In 1777 Congress expanded the standard ration for a soldier to include vinegar and sauerkraut to help stave off scurvy, with only mixed results. Arnold at the beginning of the expedition "dined at Salem [Massachusetts] where I procured two hundred pounds of ginger [to prevent scurvy]...and two hundred and seventy blankets..."[6] Ginger too was only cursorily effective against Vitamin C deficiency. As the expedition continued and supplies dwindled, scurvy would become increasingly problematic.

Dr. Senter, the expedition's physician, was only 22 at the time of the march to Quebec but would later achieve renown and respect in his chosen profession. In spite of his period acumen, he still subscribed to many of the fallacies of the day. Lamenting the loss of his medicine box with many of his medical instruments in a bateau wreck, he noted in his journal that he still retained a few surgical instruments such as "a lancet in my pocket, which enabled me at least to comply with the Sangradoine [bloodletting] method."[7] So in spite of the recognition that bad water sometimes caused dysentery, medical knowledge at the time still ordained bloodletting for many diseases and encouraged scurvy treatments that resulted in only imperfect results.

The men themselves came up with various treatments throughout the journey, again with varied results. Dearborn took an herb tea for a raging headache, concocted by his aide, with apparent alleviation of the symptoms. Later, he again "had a Violent Fever and was Delirious the Chief of the time, I had nothing to assist Nature with, but a Tea of Piggen plumb Roots, and Spruce..." This time, "my fever abated in some Degree, but did not leave me."[8] Only rest, time and food would serve to bring him back to fighting shape.

John Henry swore by his own natural medications. "In the morning when we rose, placing the edge of a broad knife at the under side of the blister [on the bark of a balsam fir tree], and my lips at the opposite part, on the back of the knife, which was declined, the liquor flowed into my mouth freely. It was heating and cordial to the stomach, attended by an agreeable pungency. This practice, which we adopted, in all likelihood contributed to the preservation of health."[9] Henry may have been at least partially right – balsam fir pitch does have varied medicinal properties that may have aided him in his continued good health.

Balsam firs were not, however, the main reason that the army maintained such overall good health. There were, indeed, two major reasons that Arnold and his men had vastly higher rates of health than other 18th century armies, despite the unimaginable feats of endurance they performed in bad weather on marginal food rations.

This was an army constantly on the move. Where most armies camped for days, weeks, or months at a time in one location, Arnold's men picked up and moved nearly every single day, only staying overnight at a given location more than once to allow others to catch up. By moving nearly every day, sanitation never became the problem it did for most armies. Latrines were only ever used once, filth did not have a chance to build up, and any waste or effluvia was swept back downstream (at least for the first half of the journey) from whence the army came, never to be encountered again. So while cases of dysentery due to poor sanitation and bad water quality did crop up, by remaining constantly in motion this disease was kept mostly at bay.

The second reason that sickness was minimized was that the sick simply could not keep up. Once they were too weak to maintain pace, they were either sent back to Fort Halifax in small groups or left at places like "Arnold's Hospital" to recuperate and later catch up. George Morison described being "touched with pity and admiration for these brave men, struggling with ruthless toil and sickness and endeavoring to conceal their situation,"[10] and continuing to march until they literally collapsed before being sent to the rear. Regardless, the result was the same. Anybody who was sick – either from sanitation or with a contagious disease – was quarantined in the most effective way and infectious viruses never were able to gain a foothold in the army.

As the expedition neared the settlements of Quebec and began to face starvation, disease and illness increased as we shall soon see in the narrative. Sometimes, however, "instead of diarrhea which tried our men most shockingly in the former part of our march, the reverse was now the complaint,"[11] when the men went for days with minimal or no sustenance. Yet Dr. Senter was occupied just as much with bumps, bruises, sprains and strains during the first half of the trip as he was with sickness. It would not be until the siege of Quebec when the army was again stationary that "the smallpox [was] all around us,"[12] and "Lice Itch, Jaundice, Crabs, Bed bugs and an unknown Sight of Fleas"[13] as well as "pleurisy, peripneumonia and other species of pulmonic complaints"[14] again took over the army. As the stationary camp outside the Quebec city walls became dirty, crowded and plagued by poor sanitation, mortality rates due to disease again returned to those of the typical army of the time.

Chapter 6: The Lower Dead River (Flagstaff Lake)

"Here the river by its extraordinary windings seemed unwilling to leave [Mount Bigelow] – two hours had passed away & we had gained nothing in our course..."[1] – Benedict Arnold

As I looked out across Flagstaff Lake from the put-in at the end of the Great Carrying Place portages, again I couldn't help but regret the changes wrought since 1775. Flagstaff Lake stands as the largest geographical change to the route since Arnold passed through. Once out in the center of the lake I peered down through the watery depths, trying to spot the original course of the Dead River, to no avail. In winter, Flagstaff Lake is partially drained and the former channel becomes partially apparent but at the height of the summer it remains hidden far below.

    I paddled west, with Mount Bigelow (named for Timothy Bigelow, one of Arnold's officers who tradition holds climbed it to gain a better view of the surrounding land) to my left and uninterrupted forest all around. In spite of being Maine's fifth largest lake, the shoreline is owned almost entirely by a combination of private land trusts, the state of Maine, and hydro-electric companies, all uninterested in development so it remains quite pristine with few power boats and little shoreline improvement. It wouldn't exist but for the dam at its northeast corner, but all things considered it's a beautiful place for paddling. In 1775, however, Arnold was several dozen feet beneath me, paddling back and forth along the meanders of the river which I now easily paddled over.

. . .

    Arnold, upon arrival at the Dead River, dashed a quick letter off to General Schuyler whom he hoped was marching towards Quebec as well. "After a very fatiguing and hazardous march over a rough country up the Kennebec river, against a very rapid stream, through an uninhabited country, and meeting with many other difficulties which we have happily surmounted, we have at last, arrived at the Dead River..."[2] He hoped to be in Quebec in fourteen days. In another note that same day he wrote to Washington that he had "twenty five

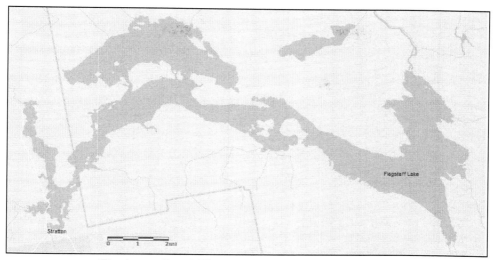
The lower Dead River: present-day Flagstaff Lake

day's provisions for the whole detachment" and that "I make no doubt of reaching the Chaudière river in eight or ten days; the greatest difficulty being, I hope already past." Per his letter, all appeared to be in good order and "the men are in high spirits."[3] His optimism, it will be seen, was misplaced in the greatest degree – it would take two weeks for the advance parties to simply reach the Chaudière and the food situation was far from secure.

The Dead River provided a much needed reprieve from the back-breaking portaging and seemingly endless upstream whitewater the expedition had faced thus far. The river "is so called from its almost seeming stagnant water"[4] tells Senter, and others agree. "The river is so remarkably still and dead, that it is difficult to determine which way it runs,"[5] wrote Abner Stocking, reveling in the luxury of easy paddling. The land "appeared to be very rich and fertile," he continued, and "wild grass covered the ground, four or five feet in height, and served us a good purpose for covering for the night."[6] Apparently some tents and blankets had been lost for several journalists by this time mention exposure to the elements during the night.

The Bigelow Mountains provided a particularly striking backdrop as they continued their journey and several journalists extolled their beauty. "On our right and left were excessively high mountains, the summits of which were covered with snow and ice. Could I have ascended to the top of one of these mountains I thought I could have overlooked all creation,"[7] yearned Stocking. Meigs made good on Stocking's wish and "set out with Capt. Hanchet to reconnoiter a very high mountain [likely one of the Bigelow Mountains]…but we were too late in the day, and returned towards evening without being able to ascend the mountain."[8] The fishing was excellent, only one very short portage blocked passage, and all in all it was a comparatively pleasurable couple of days the army spent on the lower Dead.

Navigating up the Dead, however, brought its own frustrations. "Here the river by its extraordinary windings seemed unwilling to leave [Mount Bigelow], laments Arnold "Two hours passed away & we had gained nothing in our course."[9] Some of the men, short on paddles and oars due to breakage and loss, were forced grab hold of and pull at brush and trees along the banks to make progress. The river's constricting width and twists likely inhibited even those still retaining paddles. And as the river narrowed and tributaries became more frequent, the chances of getting lost increased. "A very unlikely accident happen'd to us today, the most of our men by land miss'd their way and marched up a Small river, Which Comes into the Dead River, a few Miles a Bove where we encampt last night..."[10] moaned Dearborn. They discovered their mistake only after several miles of needless marching. The twisting stream seemed to make a mockery of their attempts at progress as it doubled and tripled back upon itself.

· · ·

As I floated over the former Dead, a small storm appeared to be brewing. During my conversation with Duluth he had warned me that the wind increases around late morning and sure enough, at 11:00 AM, the wind picked up and smatterings of rain blasted my face. True to the paddler's version of Murphy's law, no matter what direction one happens to be heading in, one will face a headwind, and indeed the waves were in my face. I hugged the north shore traveling west, and spotted three other boats in the distance riding the waves to the south of me.

By 1:00 PM, however, the sun returned and the wind died down and I was able to make better time. I took a long lunch – peanut butter and jelly per the usual – on a small beach and allowed the sun to play over my face as I dozed on shore. It was a beautiful day to be outside.

Back on the lake, I made slow but steady progress along the northern shore. Taking long, strong strokes with the paddle, I watched the resultant whirlpools scurry along the stern of the canoe before dispersing back into the lake. Speeding up my cadence, I could get the whirlpools closer together, but never managed to get one to catch up to the other. Such is the time spent on a large lake like this one.

I'd paddled and hiked through here before. I stopped in Stratton for the night in 2008 when I hiked the Appalachian Trail, spending it right on the shores of Flagstaff. Then, in 2010, I spent another night there before paddling across Flagstaff on my journey from Old Forge, NY to Fort Kent, ME along the Northern

Forest Canoe Trail. Now, in 2013, I was back in the same spot, on yet another journey. It seemed that the Stratton area is a hub for long-distance trips. It being such a pretty area, I didn't mind.

Towards mid-afternoon I caught up to another group of canoes, heading in my direction. They zigged and zagged across the water, betraying their novice paddling abilities. But the giggles trickling across the water also communicated that it didn't bother them too much.

As we came abreast of one another, I commenced the conversation. "Good afternoon. Where are you from?"

"Tufts," one girl replied. "We're a freshman orientation group." Each August, colleges throughout New England dispatch their freshman across the woods on hiking, canoeing and other outdoor trips for 2-5 days, hoping to imbue them with an appreciation for the natural wonders of New England. This was one small manifestation of that movement.

"We spent the first couple days hiking up there," another pointed towards the Bigelows, "and now we'll finish up tomorrow and head back to Boston."

Then a shriek of delighted horror escaped from the first girl. As we had neared the west end of Flagstaff, the man-made lake became shallower and shallower due to the fact that it was slowly returning to its riverine form. A wary eye was needed to navigate and ensure that no collisions with rocks or sunken debris occurred, something the newly minted freshman and novice canoeists lacked. They had just jarred against a barely submerged rock, eliciting the feminine yelp, and were now slowly spinning in circles, the rock jammed right in the center of the boat. Our conversation had come to a sudden end.

Shaking my head and giggling to myself a little bit, I continued on. Escaping a hidden rock like that in the middle of a body of water can sometimes take a while since the obstacle is centered under the boat and there are rarely other nearby solid objects from which to push off. They'd figure it out, or another boat from the group would come help. Regardless, it might be a character-building experience for them, so I waved goodbye as they ineffectually stabbed at the water with their paddles, and kept paddling. I had a hot meal cooked on a stove waiting for me.

.   .   .

Food was quickly becoming a precious resource for the members of the expedition to Quebec. Arnold had reduced rations for the army at the end of the Great Carrying Place and now most divisions were on half rations. Greene's division, temporarily in the lead after Morgan's men took on the majority of the clearing for the Great Carrying Place portages, suddenly found itself "brought to half an allowance per man". The next morning after an inventory was apparently taken, it was discovered that, "our company had but 5 or 6 pounds of flour for 60 men."[11] Greene gave orders to halt and wait for Enos to come up from behind with reserve supplies. Arnold arrived soon after on the scene and dispatched Bigelow to the back to speed the process.

It would take five days for Bigelow to return. In the meantime, Arnold "gave orders for their making cartridges"[12] from the supplies carried thus far to keep them busy. But imagine the men's surprise and consternation when Bigelow returned with only two barrels of flour, not enough to even make up for resources used while waiting. Enos himself was on half rations, so he said, as were Morgan and Meigs. It was an unfortunate situation they all found themselves in.

Historians remain confused about how this turn of events could have come about. Who was to blame for such poor provision management that rations could change from full to scant in just a couple of days? Losses on the Kennebec due to leaky and wrecked bateaux certainly hurt the situation, and the dispersed nature of the divisions made management tough. The finger is naturally pointed at Arnold himself as chief administrator in addition to commander, and most of the fault is likely his. It should be noted, however, that the unique challenges faced in leading a wilderness expedition exacerbated an already challenging administration job, which however, is inexcusable given the situation the army now found themselves in. Food continued to be shuffled between divisions in small amounts to help make up deficits, but all were now conscience of the issue and began to hold onto their allotments tighter.

One anticipated complication around this time turned out to be the reverse. Greene while waiting for requisitions, was camped just past the cabin and homestead of Natanis who, if the reader remembers, was known as a British spy to Arnold. Arnold had ordered that Natanis be killed on sight by John Henry's scouting part. Henry described their first appearance on the scene, several days prior, when still way in front of the main body. "We landed some miles below where we supposed his house was...We arrived at the house of Natanis, after a march, probably of three miles...Approaching on all sides with the utmost circumspection, we ran quickly to the cabin, our rifles prepared, and in full belief that we had caught Natanis." But Natanis was not at home, as Henry narrated. "The bird was flown. He was wiser and more adroit than his assailants, as you will afterwards learn."[13]

Confident that Natanis was gone, Henry and the scouting party had looked around. "The house was prettily placed on a bank twenty feet high," and, "for an Indian cabin, was clean and tight,"[14] he extolled, unwilling to give unqualified admiration but nonetheless appreciating its construction and situation.

Later events would show that Natanis, far from being a British spy, was in fact a friend to the patriot cause. Why he told Colburn's scouts back in August that he was a British spy remains unclear, but Henry tells of the aid that Natanis gave the scouts soon after the attempted ambush at his house. "As we were going along in uncertainty, partly inclined to take the western stream, one of the party fortunately saw a strong stake which had been driven down at the edge of the water, with a piece of neatly folded birch bark, inserted into a split at the top."[15] It was a map, drawn by Natanis, making clear the route to the Height of Land. The scouting party made valuable use of it, and later the following army did the same. Natanis would later identify himself to Arnold on the Chaudière and participate in the attack on Quebec, proving to be a valuable ally.

    This would be one of the few pieces of good luck in what was only becoming a worsening situation. The weather continued to deteriorate as winter approached ever faster. Haskell tell us it was "A rainy day…Uncomfortable weather" on October 19th, 'Thick weather and rainy" on the 20th, and by the 21st it "continues wet and stormy."[16] The night of October 21st many were camped near where the modern day town of Stratton, Maine sits, close to where the North Branch of the Dead River enters Flagstaff Lake. The men went to bed in the muck and mire after three days of heavy downpour, wet and bedraggled. "In the evening a most heavy torrent of rain fell upon us, which continued all night…We slept soundly" remembered John Henry. They chose for a campsite "a bank eight or nine feet high,"[17] but it would prove to be not high enough. Arnold also remembered having "slept very comfortably until 4 o clock" when all of a sudden, hell broke loose. The heavy rain caused the river to leave its banks. "We were awakened by the freshet which came rushing on us like a torrent, having rose 8 feet perpendicular in 9 hours…"[18] Forced to scramble for higher ground dragging their gear behind them, they "passed the remainder of the night in no very agreeable situation. Senter noted dryly, "From a Dead River it had now become live enough."[19] The increased current and flooded conditions would only add to their woes.

    . . .

    I passed over both Natanis' cabin and the site where Arnold and much of the army scrambled for higher ground to avoid floodwaters as I worked my way towards my only night indoors for the trip. Where Arnold passed one of the worst nights of the expedition I would spend the most luxurious of my trip.

    As I neared the west end of Flagstaff, two paddlers in a canoe rounded the corner of one of the islands. They kept up a fast pace and faint, periodic "hups" drifted across the water as paddles dipped in time and they switched sides at brief intervals. It was my friends John and his wife Patty.

    "That you, Sam?" John called.

    "Fancy meeting you out here!" I joked across the water.

    I struggled mightily to keep up with their pace as I followed them to their house. They slowed to a gentler speed only to pull away as we neared their dock. "Show-offs!" I hollered from behind. If I couldn't keep up, at least I could trash talk a little.

I showered and cleaned off the gunk from six days on the water. We ate spaghetti with homemade sauce complete with meatballs and sausage. I took a mountainous portion and enjoyed every bite, washing it down with dark beer, as I told them about my journey so far. They were amazed at the distance I had come to date but I laughed it off. "It's just me out here. There's nothing to do in camp so I might as well keep paddling. It's no fun talking to yourself, and besides, folks think you're crazy if you do it too much."

It was wonderful to have somebody to yak with over the meal – solitary meals are all well and good but the conversation frequently lags. Afterwards we sat on the porch and looked out towards the river as night darkened. Crickets chirped peacefully and the occasional bullfrog let out a croak. As I turned in that night, snuggled down in a warm bed between clean sheets, I couldn't help but be thankful for the dry night, fresh bedding, and full belly of the 21st century. Life was good.

Interlude: The Expedition's Interactions with American Indians

"I have several times, on my march, wrote you by the Indians, some of whom have returned and brought no answer. I am apprehensive they have betrayed me."[1] – Benedict Arnold

Benedict Arnold and the men who accompanied him through the Maine wilderness had extremely polarized relations with American Indians. On the one hand was their innate prejudice, symptomatic of almost all colonists on the North American continent, and on the other was their very real need for their services as guides, scouts and messengers for the expedition, jobs that no white man could do as effectively due to the American Indians' familiarity with the woods and comprehensive camp craft skills. This disconnect between prejudice against and need for the American Indians make for some sometimes contradictory statements by the journalists.

When Arnold asked Colburn to send out scouts pre-expedition, he scoffed at the resultant report because it came from "a noted villain and very little credit I am told, is to be given to his information."[2] What is the point of sending out scouts if you don't trust the resulting report? Later, after Henry had met Natanis and realized his patriotism, he was able to ask with a straight face, "Why did you not speak to your friends?" to the man he had earlier tried to ambush. Natanis' natural response was, "You would have killed me,"[3] which he likely said while shaking his head at the white man's folly.

Two incidents exemplify this contradiction in how the expedition interacted with the American Indians it met and employed along the route. The first is the case of Eneas "a faithful Indian"[4] and Sabattis, two of the original American Indians who set out with Arnold. Joining them were Frederick Jaquin, a colonist of French descent and John Hall, a British deserter who spoke French. The four were sent "with Letters to some Gentlemen in Quebec,"[5] including John Mercier, a patriotic contact of Arnold's in Quebec with a request for all available information on the defendants and armaments of Quebec City. They set out from the Great Carrying Place ahead of the army. The letter eventually fell into enemy hands and Mercier was arrested by Governor Guy Carleton. But how? Was it by pure accident or was some member of the messenger party a traitor?

In spite of branding Eneas "a faithful Indian", Arnold's suspicions immediately turned to one of the American Indians, lamenting in following letters to Mercier that "My letter of the 13th, I sent by an Indian, who I believe has betrayed me,"[6] and to Montgomery, bringing forces to Quebec via Montreal that, "I wrote Gen. Schuyler, the 13th of October, by an Indian, I thought trusty, enclosed to my friend in Quebec...I make no doubt he has betrayed my trust."[7] Given the choice between an American Indian he originally thought faithful and a former British soldier who might naturally be suspected, Arnold "make[s] no doubt" that it was Eneas who is the traitor. Yet contemporary accounts tell us that indeed it was John Hall. Safe in his cover as a British deserter and unsuspected by Arnold, he returns to the army and is captured months later in the failed assault on Quebec. There, an escape plan by many of the prisoners is foiled at the last minute by the same John Hall as James Melvin tells us. "Our scheme found out; the sentry hearing some noise in the cellar, search was made, and some suspicion raised which might have passed off, had not one of our own men, JOHN HALL, discovered the whole affair, and all the sergeants and corporals were put in irons. [Capitalization Melvin's]"[8] Had Arnold suspected the correct traitor, the later jailbreak may have gone off successfully and perhaps saved some of the dozens who later died in captivity.

The second anecdote of course involves Natanis. Suspicion of his British allegiance allegedly came from his own mouth when he told Colburn's scouts that he was in the pay of Carleton and the British. It was a natural thing, therefore, that Arnold ordered Natanis, "both as rogueish and malicious as ever existed,"[9] shot on sight by John Henry and the scouting party. He too, however, proved to be a friend. As has already been noted, he left the scouting party a map directing them to the proper branch of the Dead River and may even have helped them find their way through the swamps surrounding Lac Megantic later in the expedition. He made himself known to the army on the Chaudière River, walking up to John Henry and then, "shook hands in the way of an old acquaintance,"[10] doubtless with a twinkle in his eye while doing so. He told Henry he had tailed them since their first appearance on the Dead, keeping a watchful eye on the expedition. Now that he had made himself known, he joined the army for the remainder of the march and was wounded in the attack on Quebec.

Two different American Indians, then, were suspected of foul play but in the end proved friendly, and indeed many others were essential to the completion of the expedition. Arnold's journal and letters peppered with references to letters sent "by an Indian."[11] Their superior paddling and small boat skills enabled them to quickly ferry between the diverse divisions spread out over the march, allowing Arnold to communicate with his division commanders. Arnold himself traveled in a dugout for much of the journey, paddled by American Indians, which allowed him to maneuver quickly as well and he used that boat or a similar one on the Chaudière to speed ahead and send back relief for his starving men, again paddled by American Indians. Near the French settlements, Arnold "met with two Penobscot Indians who appeared friendly & assisted us over the Portage."[12] Overall, American Indians appeared to be very well disposed towards the Americans. The army made use of American Indian portage trails and campsites, saving themselves some hard clearing work, and even co-opted several canoes discovered hidden in the underbrush for their own uses. Dearborn found two near the Height of Land and Arnold snagged one as well on Lac Megantic. American Indians served as guides, scouts, and couriers for Arnold, and in spite of their small numbers on the expedition had an outsized impact on its successfully reaching Quebec.

Once among the French inhabitants, Arnold even attempted to recruit additional American Indians to assist his small army of weary men in the attack on Quebec. He made a speech to assembled natives among the Quebec settlements, saying "a new king and his wicked great men want to take our lands and money without our consent…we hear the French and Indians in Canada have sent to us, that the king's troops oppress them and make them pay a great price for their [goods]; press them to take up arms…By the desire of the French and Indians, our brothers, we have come to their assistance…If the Indians, our brethren, will join us, we will be very much obliged to them…"[13] It was a clever speech laden with flattery and promises of money and food and fifty American Indians soon signed on with their canoes. This was a controversial move for Europeans did not condone using American Indians in war, deeming it as "uncivilized", Henry calling it a "horrible system of aggression which…astonished and disgusted the civilized world."[14] It was only the second time American Indians had taken a direct part in the war and while their participation did not affect the outcome, it was a harbinger of things to come. American Indian tribes would ally themselves on both sides in the conflict throughout the colonies. Regardless of with whom they sided, it rarely boded well for North America's first inhabitants in the end.

Yet for all this, the prejudices of the era remained and throughout the expedition, the men were warned to beware of the American Indian presence. "We frequently saw ducks etc. and many moose deer yet we discharged not a gun," remembers John Henry (before they were desperate enough to shoot and eat anything). "In truth we had been made to believe that this country had numerous Indians in it."[15] The historical clashes along the colonies' frontier and vast cultural differences between the patriots and American Indians caused a strong element of suspicion and distrust between them to remain.

Chapter 7: North Branch of the Dead River and the Chain of Ponds

"The rapidity of the current renders it almost impossible for the Battoes to ascend the River, or the men to find their way...our Provisions almost exhausted, & incessant rains for three days...so that we have but a melancholy prospect before us, but in general in high spirits."[1] – Benedict Arnold

I woke the next morning and took a minute to revel in the sheets and blankets around me. Nothing feels so good as a warm bed after sleeping on the ground for a while. But I wasn't going to ascend the North Branch of the Dead by lying there, so I rolled off the mattress, dressed in my foul-smelling clothes, and slipped out the door before John or Patty rose.

I met Duluth Wing at the local diner. He pulled up in his pick-up truck and stepped out, a short, sprightly man who belied his 85 years with a quick wit and strong step. He did have a bit of a paunch which, when later a friend complimented his wife's cooking, he noted it as the direct cause of his widening belt line. "It's too good," he said then. But I was just meeting him at the Stratton Diner.

"You must be Sam," he greeted me as he stepped down from the driver's seat. "You've made good time."

We quickly began to discuss the trip and, like any old-timer with an audience, he began to share tales from his own trips along the route in the 1970's. I was thrilled to be that audience.

"When we came to Wyman Lake, it was full of pulpwood. Just carpeted. We couldn't paddle through it, of course, so we stopped and passed the time with the dam operator. We were chatting away when I noticed the canoe drifting downstream – we hadn't tied it up well enough, or the water rose. I had to run down to the river, and wade in after it. But I got it!" he chuckled.

"But you're done with that part now. Up the North Branch, it is now for you."

I agreed, all ears. "How'd you cross the border Duluth?"

He laughed again. They, like me, had felt it important to carry the canoe every inch of the route under their own power. So his paddling partner, Cecil Pierce, took the canoe and carried it across the border (the border follows the

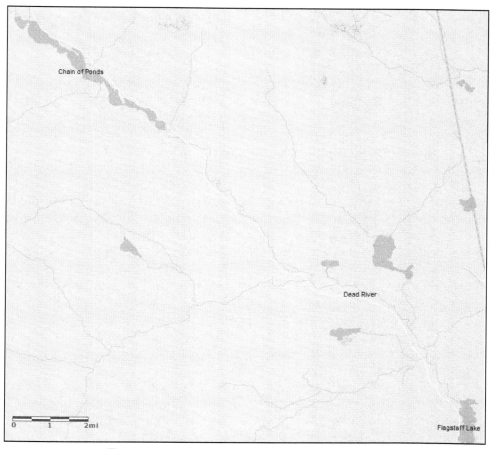

The upper Dead River and the Chain of Ponds

height of land so a long portage is needed to cross it, as we shall see later in the narrative).

"So I followed him in the truck, just inching along the shoulder of the road while he walked with the canoe. When we got to the border, we had a pretty funny conversation with Border Patrol. 'Why doesn't he just get in the truck?' they asked me! They never really did understand what we were doing."

It was fine listening to Duluth's stories, but we were standing in the parking lot. So after a bit we hopped in his truck and drove briefly down the road to the local museum, the Dead River Area Historical Society. Devoted to mostly memorabilia from pre-Flagstaff Lake (the damming of the river flooded three small villages and forcibly removed large numbers of residents), a smaller portion is dedicated to the Arnold Expedition. Duluth has been the prime mover behind collecting many of the artifacts housed here.

As we navigated among the displays, Duluth kept up a running commentary about each of the artifacts.

"This here is a medicinal spoon. Found this at the Hospital Site – which is not where you portaged, by the way. It is further north along the shore of East Carry Pond. And some buttons from uniforms. These here, do you know what these are? These are setting pole spikes – go on the bottom of setting poles."

I could only shake my head in wonder at all the stuff he had found in the woods. He told me he goes out with a metal detector for hours, roaming over the route and hoping for a ping.

"One day, I had found nothing. I'd been looking for hours and not a thing. Then, I leaned up against this big old tree, about to turn in for the day, when the detector starts going crazy." He points to a large pile of musket balls. "I found these all together, right at the base of that tree: 832 musket balls. Some soldier, exhausted from carrying them, must have set down the bag here as he rested and just left them. They were all jumbled on top of each other, just setting there pretty as you please. Bag of course rotted away but they were there."

I took a number of pictures of the displays and we walked around for a long time, looking at it all. To think, 240 years ago this stuff was being used by Arnold and his men, traveling the same route I now am. It was a very inspiring experience for me.

Finally, however, I decided it was time to get back on the water. Duluth waited for me while I ran into the grocery store to grab some supplies and then drove me back to John and Patty's place. After the requisite pictures Duluth shoved a bag into my hand. "From my wife," he said gruffly. "She thought you might need something sweet to keep you going."

I stammered my thanks, climbed into my canoe, and was off under a warm sun and clear skies. I couldn't have asked for nicer hosts in John and Patty or a more willing friend and teacher than Duluth. It was a wonderful stop.

· · ·

The expedition, however, faced a very different situation as dawn arrived on October 22nd. Arnold made a gross understatement in his journal when he said, "This morning presented us a very disagreeable prospect, the Country round entirely overflowed."[2] The river had risen somewhere between eight and ten feet overnight and it was no longer a stream confined to a channel but instead a fast flowing sheet of water that had spread across much of the surrounding land. It would take hours or in some cases days for the men to regroup and find any gear that had not sunk or floated away.

Once they finally resumed their march, the men were forced to resort to all sorts of measures to make forward progress. Men pulling themselves up hand over hand via littoral bushes became the norm. "Such a horrid current as rendered it impossible to proceed in any other method than by hauling the bateaux up by the bushes, painters, &c."[3] wrote Senter. Attempts to paddle the bateaux resulted in numerous disasters. "At this place the stream is very rapid, in passing which, five or six battoes filled and overset, by which we lost several barrels of provisions, a number of guns, some clothes and cash."[4] Boats that were already on their last legs fell to pieces and others were destroyed as the current swept them against rocks, necessitating the overloading of remaining bateaux. Progress was exceptionally slow.*

    The detachments marching along the shore faced an even tougher challenge. "One of the most fatigueing Marches we had as yet performed tho the distance was not great in a direct line,"[5] wrote one tired walker. The men were forced to make long detours away from the main river simply to circumvent what had formerly been small tributaries but were now raging torrents. "The small rivulets (and they were not few) were swelled to an enormous size, as obliged the land party to trace them up for many miles till a narrow part offered, and then could only cross by felling large trees over them,"[6] described Senter, clearly in some awe at the changes the storm had wrought. Meigs ably summed up the travails of making progress against the current when he wrote "Our whole course this day only 4 miles,"[7] and Senter with another dry aside wrote that, "our progression was exceedingly gradual."[8]

    Yet the men had no choice but to continue to press forward. To wait days or weeks for the current to subside would have meant disaster given their limited food supplies and the worsening weather.

    Winter was nearly upon them. "It continued raining & snowing all night…Ab[out] two inches now on the ground," wrote Arnold on October 24th and the next day it "Snowed and blowed very hard."[9] Senter summed up the weather when he wrote "Every prospect of distress now came thundering on with a two fold rapidity. A storm of snow had covered the ground of nigh six inches deep, attended with very severe weather."[10] For men whose clothing was quickly becoming rags and whose shoes were falling off their feet (if still present at all), these were dim prospects indeed.

    The food situation was still worse. All were on half rations now, and some faced even greater restrictions in their daily diet. While they were not out of food yet, they had begun to attempt to supplement their meager rations with

---

* The reference to lost "cash" here has resulted in an interesting side note. According to Meigs – quoted above – and Morison who states that "a large sum of money destined to pay off the men [was lost]." (Roberts, *March*, p. 517) some amount of money was indeed lost, perhaps a significant amount. Various theories have popped up for where it has ended up. One idea has it that two guides for the expedition returned several years later and found it, using it to purchase large amounts of land. However, it may still be out there, awaiting some future treasure hunter.

items that traditionally are not considered food stuffs. "I found them destitute any eatable whatever, except a few candles, which were used for supper and breakfast the next morning, by boiling them in water gruel,"[11] remembers the doctor as he came upon a small group of men one evening. The day of the flood Caleb Haskell "had nothing to eat,"[12] but two days later somewhere found more provisions. Since they didn't know when they might find relief, some likely began to exaggerate their food situation and their journals betrayed their fears. "We are in an absolute danger of starving,"[13] dreaded Topham. Arnold may have been exaggerating in the other direction when he wrote on the 24th, two days after the storm, that "We are now reduced to 12 or 15 days [of half-rations]."[14] Regardless of exactly how much food was left, they needed to find relief quickly. As Arnold noted when he wrote that "… we have but a melancholy prospect before us, but in general in high spirits," however, they managed to keep their morale up. "I hope for the best,"[15] Topham wrote soon after, and many (though not all, as we shall soon see) shared his positive outlook.

. . .

Worried about my making a similar mistake to Arnold, several people including Duluth had warned me to make sure I headed up the North Branch of the Dead, not the South like some of Arnold's men did in 1775. It was an easy thing to avoid with my modern maps and I made my way through the final vestiges of flooded Flagstaff Lake before regaining the river's current and heading upstream.

The lower North Branch was fairly tame and I was enjoying my paddle through the twists and turns of the smaller river, passing woods on my right and the occasional house on my left, when a voice hailed me.

"Are you Sam?"

"Sam I am," I responded, patting myself on the back for my cleverness and searching briefly for the voice's origin before spotting a man up on a deck doing some carpentry. "Who are you and how do I know you?"

"You just spent the morning with my father," Duluth's son responded. "He told me to keep an eye out for you. Good luck!"

I waved in thanks and moved on towards a short portage around Eustis Dam.

Ledge Falls followed soon after, which for no good reason except its name I understood to be a short ledge drop. I paddled up to just what I expected – a short ledge drop – which I portaged around on some rocks. A bony set of rapids followed which I lined up to a bend in the river. Around that bend – more rocky rapids and ledges! Examining my options here, I wasn't thrilled with the choices. The shores were lined with thick scrub brush and alders which appeared impassable. But the river was far too shallow to make any progress in the boat.

So I elected to compromise and, loading the boat and gear on my back, portaged up the middle of the stream.

This turned out to be a terrible idea. While the ledges themselves were fairly dry and knobby enough to get a purchase on, every time I sloshed through a puddle of water, I nearly broke my neck. River stone gets its reputation for a reason and trying to keep purchase on the smooth, alga-covered rocks just barely submerged beneath the river's surface was too much for me. I stumbled and slid my way for a hundred yards or so, stubbing toes and barking shins while cursing all the while, before throwing in the towel. A new plan was needed.

I found one short section of water just deep enough so I lined for a short distance. But it soon became too rocky again so I was finally forced to choose the only option remaining to me. I picked river left and portaged through the woods, forcing my way through a thicket of alders for several hundred yards. Branches lashed across my face and caught at my ankles. Several times I became stuck and had to laboriously back up, sight unseen, to pick a slightly new route that would allow the canoe through. It felt like ages before I finally reached the upper end of Ledge Falls. In the end, it was perhaps half a mile long – certainly not the short drop I had expected.

The issue was that I was having the opposite problem that Arnold had. The river was so low and boney now in August that anywhere there was a significant drop in elevation, the river simply became too shallow to paddle. I was forced to either line or portage. Portaging required tough bushwhacking but lining left something to be desired as well since there was so little water in which to float the boat. While it was certainly better than a raging torrent and snow, I would have gladly settled for a happy medium.

This kind of canoe tripping was not new to me. As I took a break at the north end of this most recent portage, I laughed to myself as I reflected back on other portages like it, on other trips. I learned to paddle and canoe trip at a boys summer camp in Vermont called Keewaydin. A traditional summer camp with sports, dramatics, archery and camping, it places a large emphasis on canoe trips. Starting with short two- or three-day trips for the youngest boys, by the time they reach age sixteen campers can take thirty-day trips to northern Quebec. I had spent several years at the camp as a camper and several more guiding some of those same trips. While the younger boys travel through popular canoeing territory that has portage trails and campsites, the oldest boys travel to lands too remote to have any sign of human impact.

It was a portage on one of those Quebec trips that I always remember at times like this one. It was towards the end of a long day, replete with numerous portages. Most portages are bushwhacks up there, and this one was no different. Somehow, I managed to get the bow of the canoe stuck in a fir tree, and with it still on my shoulders, no amount of pushing, pulling or wrenching would free it. I was tired and thirsty and I was in no mood for a small tree to give the kind of trouble it seemed to be giving me. But with my fury mounting, I likely only managed to wedge it harder (remember, I don't like to put the canoe down mid-portage and that was only too true at age sixteen). But stuck as I was, I had no choice so I finally threw the canoe to the ground. I was blind with anger and it's the only time that I remember where I was literally "hopping mad". I jumped up and down, just like in the cartoons, cursing and yelling at the canoe. Since then, I've managed to realize that that probably wasn't worth getting that angry about, but I still think back to that time whenever I finish a tough carry. It's a benchmark for me – no portage can ever be as tough as that one seemed.

My only night on the North Branch was one of the more pleasant I spent on the trip. The upper reaches of this river and the Chain of Ponds which directly followed would be some of the most remote sections of the route. While there was some faint road noise from nearby Route 27, I found a balsam fir grove with a wide open understory, plenty of firewood, and no cabins or houses nearby. Spreading my gear out and relaxing around the fire, a peace swept over me that clean sheets simply can't evoke. It was good to be back in the woods.

It would also be one of the most luxurious meals of the trip – Fresh out of town, I ate steak and a baked potato roasted in the coals as well as baked beans followed by some of Mrs. Wing's sweets. As I settled in for the night I was the picture of contentment. It's good to be king.

The morning of my eighth day of the trip, I arrived at Shadagee Falls. While in 2013 it appeared as only another set of rapids requiring more poling, lining or portaging, in 1775 it was the site of an event of far more portent.

. . .

On the evening of October 23rd, 1775, near Shadagee Falls, Arnold called for a council of war to determine how (and if) the expedition was to proceed. Attending were Benedict Arnold, Major Return Meigs, and Captains Morgan, Smith and Hendricks as well as their lesser officers. Absent were Greene and Enos who were too far behind to attend. The expedition was in a tough situation and Arnold needed to know that his officers were behind him. They were camped on a dry spit of land, later named "Camp Disaster", where they would decide the future of the expedition.

Importantly, the vote was unanimous to move forward. None of these officers would back down, and Arnold no doubt urged them on with promises that relief was closer by moving forward than by turning back. It was understood at this meeting, (though whether it was true, historians are still unsure), that Enos still had numerous reserves of provisions that would be distributed upon arrival. It was also decided here to dispatch all invalids and those too sick to travel back to Fort Western – twenty-six men in all. Finally, Captain Hanchett was sent forward with fifty picked men to make all haste to the nearest settlements and "forward on provisions from the French inhabitants."[16] Greene and Enos were both sent letters, ordering them upon "receipt of this you should proceed with as many of the best men of your division as you can furnish with 15 day's provisions; and that the remainder whether sick or well, should be immediately sent back to the commissary."[17] Arnold, "our gallant colonel himself, after admonishing us to persevere as he hitherto had done,"[18] soon followed Hanchett to find relief for his beleaguered men, little knowing that his orders to Enos would be the subject of much debate later on.

Greene and Enos with their officers held their own council of war the next day, unaware of the meeting or decisions of the forward divisions. The verdict was much different. While Greene and his officers all voted to continue onwards and catch Arnold, Enos' officers voted to return. Enos himself "Declared to us [that] he was willing to go and …share the same fate with us, But was obliged to tarry thro' the means of his Effeminate officers."[19] He would return with his men, all the while professing his desire to press onwards. Later he was charged with orchestrating the whole charade, being really in favor of returning with his men the whole time.

Proof of his disingenuousness is perhaps given when, instead of the promised six barrels of provisions to be given to Greene he gave only two. Thayer, in charge of requisitioning provisions from Enos, said "it is surprising that the party returning, professing Christianity, should prove so ill-disposed toward their fellow-brethren and soldiers, in the situation we were in, and especially when we observe our numerous wants, and the same time they overflowing in abundance of all sorts, and far more than what was necessary for their return."[20] Enos' actions would result in a court-martial immediately upon his return which, since Arnold and the army was still in Quebec at the time, resulted in his being exonerated of all charges. The only witnesses were his own officers who had returned with him.

Greene and his men continued onwards while, "with tears in his Eyes, [Enos] took, as he then suppos'd and absolutely thought, his last farewell of [Greene's divison]."[21] Thayer, who narrates this event, appeared dubious of Enos' sincerity and posterity has mostly agreed with him since. Most men considered that Enos had the easiest job of all divisions since "the advantage of the arrangement was conspicuous as the rear division would not only have the roads cut, rivers cleared passible for boats... [but] encampments formed and the bough huts remaining."[22] The fact that they turned back while refusing to share their surplus provisions only further infuriated the men who continued to battle onwards. "That they therefore should be the first to turn back excited in us much manly resentment,"[23] fumed Abner Stocking and many others agreed. In the stroke of one evening Arnold had lost 450 men and some badly needed food. It would have severe repercussions for their assault on Quebec.

. . .

Nothing of Camp Disaster or that momentous evening remained at Shadagee Falls. The birds chirped and the river burbled, just like everywhere else, so, with nothing holding me there, I continued upstream. The rest of the North Branch continued to get narrower and shallower and I spent the morning of my eighth day in and out of the boat continuously. Sometimes I portaged, sometimes I lined or dragged, occasionally I poled, but rarely did I paddle. The final kilometer to the southern end of Lower Pond – the first of the Chain of Ponds – was nearly continuous walking since the stream (as it was more aptly described now) was too shallow and steep to do much else. But I finally arrived at Lower Pond. My oft-bruised toes were thankful.

A dam now retains a significant amount of water in the Chain of Ponds, something that Arnold of course did not have the benefit of. This meant that between Bog Pond and Long Pond I was able to paddle where Arnold was forced to portage.

The Chain of Ponds – five named ponds in all below Horseshoe Stream and then another four named after the stream, were a stunning respite from the upstream haul. A slight headwind blew in my face but the scenery was breathtaking. Steep hillsides on either side dropped straight down to the water, forming a V-shaped valley, the far end of which appeared to drop off the face of the earth. Clouds scuttled by overhead and an ominous looking darker bank threatened to the west. I felt a peaceful sense of insignificance as the heavens painted an ever-changing panorama in front of me.

Lunch was on a small beach on Natanis Pond (not to be confused with the Natanis of our story, this was named for a female American Indian of a later time). I stopped in briefly at a small campground to borrow the phone – cell service was non-existent this far into the mountains and I didn't want Elizabeth to call Search & Rescue for me. The owner was a short, round woman with a matching personality – exuding warmth and conviviality. "Well if that isn't just the neatest adventure you're on," she told me when I described the trip. She vowed to learn more about Arnold.

The campground was set on a narrow peninsular jutting into the pond and some of Arnold's men camped there in 1775. Any remnants are covered up by RV hook-ups and iron fire pits so I lost no time exploring but continued paddling. The storm was threatening overhead and the upcoming waters had me worried about navigation.

Duluth had given me some fairly detailed advice for navigating Horseshoe Stream between Round Pond and Arnold Pond, all of which proved invaluable. From Round Pond, I entered a likely looking inlet to the southwest, looking for the outlet of Horseshoe Stream. But it quickly dead-ended. Searching among some lily pads and algae further north, I discovered the outlet. It was on the northwest side of the pond as Duluth had told me. From then on, I vowed to follow his guidance.

Horseshoe Stream itself began deep and debris-free but quickly became clogged with overhanging branches, strainers, and beaver dams. More dragging! I navigated through its many twists and turns, sometimes backtracking when I discovered an impassable channel and selecting another. It was a pleasant paddle among the alders and reeds, with birds abounding. Lots of evidence of beavers surrounded me but none surfaced to say "Hi". I was worried that I might mistake the stream draining Hathan Bog from the north for the main channel but it was quite obvious when I came to it and I was able to stay on the correct route.

The threatening storm by this time was sending the occasional wave of rain across my bow – the first rain I had had while awake besides a few drops on Middle Carry Pond – and at one point I quickly got off the water as lightning struck a little too close for comfort. But a little rain hurts no one and it certainly didn't slow me down.

Duluth's directions stated that upon finding the junction with Hathan Stream, I should look to the west for a tall esker that runs parallel to the stream. When I arrived I laughed a little to myself – the esker would be tough to miss. On the other side lay Lost Pond.

Lost Pond is aptly named. When historian Justin Smith – the first to give a detailed examination of the journals in order to accurately map the army's route – was doing research he was confused by the apparent presence of an extra body of water described in Arnold's journal that he couldn't find on the ground. Only after miles of tramping over the territory with local guides did he eventually stumble on Lost Pond. Because it drains only a tiny basin, there is no outlet channel and it only flows in the spring or after heavy rains. There is no reason to suspect its presence on the other side of the high esker and one guesses that the only reason Arnold stumbled across it was that the army, with its cumbersome bateaux, was desperate to escape the shallow and convoluted Horseshoe Stream. But it was through Lost Pond that Arnold went so it was through Lost Pond that I would go.

I portaged there via a steep game trail up and over the esker and into Lost Pond, not much more than fifty meters. After what felt like only a dozen paddle strokes I arrived at the end of the small body of water and took out at the north end. Here I again regained the top of the esker with the canoe on my shoulders and was able to take advantage of Duluth's hard work.

A game trail follows the top of the esker for much of the way and Duluth, aided by a hand saw and pair of clippers, had widened the trail and flagged it with orange survey tape to permit travel. While no one else had yet made use of the trail besides Duluth and myself, it was in excellent shape and I couldn't help but send up a silent 'thank you' to Duluth back in Stratton for his dedication and effort.

Following the tape I arrived after perhaps 500 meters on a logging road. Another ½ kilometer brought me to a bridge over Horseshoe Stream. I put in there for lack of a better option and it was only a hop, skip and a jump of further of dragging before I arrived at Horseshoe Pond.

Horseshoe Pond was blanketed with lily pads – water was barely visible in most places. I periodically looked behind me as I parted the greenery, watching the narrow channel I created by forcing my way through them.

The last two portages are best termed bushwhacks. Arnold noted that "All these small Lakes have a communication with each other by a small Brook or river, & between most of them are considerable Falls, which occasions so many Portages."[24] He was correct when terming them "brooks" – they were definitely not navigable and even in 2013 there was clearly no travel between any of them except by portage. I found an old woods road for part of the way between Horseshoe and Mud – Duluth had again alerted me to its possible presence - but simply forced my way through thick balsam firs to get from Mud to Arnold. I had made it to the end of the Chain of Ponds.

.   .   .

Back at the head of the North Branch of the Dead with Arnold, the dam at the south end of Lower Pond was of course not yet built in 1775. This meant that the ponds which fed the North Branch were much more variable in their water levels and, in spite of the heavy rains Arnold had seen, meant that he had one more portage to do than I did.

In the grand scheme of things, it didn't matter. One less portage would not have improved things. The men were hungry, cold, and exhausted. More importantly, their morale was beginning to drop as they worried if they would ever find their way out of the wilderness. It was snowing again and "the ground [was] covered with a pretty deep snow which had fell in the night…in consequence, our progress was much impeded."[25] They were about equi-distant from the nearest English or French settlements meaning that they were as far as they would ever be from help. It was not an enviable situation to be in.

In spite of this, the men were still able to experience a little bit of the same sense of awe that I felt while traversing the Chain of Ponds. "We entered a lake surrounded by high and craggy mountains, and perpendicular rocks of very considerable altitude which about 11 o'clock, A.M. cast us into a dusky shade." Henry was so awestruck that he commented that the area had a "resemblance to the vale of death,"[26] which his compatriots immediately began to tease him about, but it is demonstrative of the power of the place. Arnold himself was clearly a little awestruck when he wrote that "All these lakes are surrounded with a chain of prodigious high mountains."[27] It was, and is, a unique place.

After navigating the lower ponds, they came to Horseshoe Stream where they too had a little trouble finding the outlet to Horseshoe Stream. "Here we were a long time at a Los for the Portage – at length we found a small brook which we entered & rowed up ab[out] 1 ½ miles with much difficulty." They too encountered snags and beaver dams and were "obliged to Clear away drift Loggs in many places."[28] Arnold camped somewhere along Horseshoe Stream in what must have been a tight and uncomfortable spot for there is little high or open ground in the region.

They appear to have found Lost Pond with less trouble than either Justin Smith or I had – perhaps the intervening years have made it less obvious – and by the time Meigs got there with his division they were ready to camp for the night which they did "on the northwest side, upon a high hill, which is a carrying-place."[28] I may have walked over the very site as I regained the esker to portage into Horseshoe Pond. Duluth's trail likely crosses either through or quite close to it. Meigs too was amazed to be so near the mountains.

The last few portages between Horseshoe, Mud, and Arnold Ponds appear to have changed little in the intervening years. The brooks between were "incapable of floating the batteaux,"[30] wrote Senter, and again the men cut trails to permit the portaging of the remaining boats.

Senter wrote that he ate "the jawbone of a swine destitute of any covering," for breakfast the morning he reached Arnold Pond. "This we boiled in a quantity of water, that with a little thickening constituted our sumptuous eating."[31] Others like Abner Stocking, however, "caught plenty of trout"[32] so that at least some were not yet resorting to Senter's methods. Time would tell that there were at least some provisions still available to the men.

Morale suffered an additional setback as news began to trickle forwards that Enos and his men had turned back. No doubt the mountains rang with curses aimed at those with less fortitude. But, at least according to the journalists, in the end it only pushed them onwards to endure more. The men who were sent back due to illness or injury "returned with heavy hearts. They lamented that their indisposition prevented them from sharing in this grand advance throughout, since they had contributed to its success thus far."[33] Indeed, the men who continued forward were "fired with more than Hannibalian enthusiasm." As they trundled out of the woods from the final portage to Arnold Pond, "a beautiful one upon the height of land from where the Dead River takes its rise," the men felt unstoppable. Neither "American Alps, nor Pyrenees were obstacles,"[34] wrote Senter, continuing his Hannibal metaphor. It was all downhill from here, though additional hardships would yet rear their heads.

. . .

By the time I myself emerged onto Arnold Pond, it was pouring rain and nearing six o-clock. I had portaged half a dozen times and while the total distance didn't add up to much, the challenging terrain and often non-existent trail made them tough in their own right. As I finished the final portage into Arnold Pond, the rain suddenly eased and a ray of sunshine poked through. I knew it was time to camp, and with the heavens shining down on me as if to say, "Nice job," I set up my tent and ate dinner on the shores of Arnold Pond. Whereas Arnold was still unsure of time and distance to relief for his men, I had a full stomach and knew where I was. While he hurried ahead of the main body of the army towards help, I was able to peacefully watch swallows swoop over the calm waters, catching bugs after the storm. I felt both literally and figuratively on top of the world – it was all downstream for me as well, though I too had one or two more unexpected obstacles to face myself.

The author standing in front of Colburn House, construction site of Arnold's bateaux and present day home of the Arnold Expedition Historical Society

A typical beautiful day on the lower Kennebec. A wide river, its many shallow stretches provided challenges for both Arnold and the author

Portaging through the Great Carrying Place. Arnold's men made as many as seven or eight trips over a single portage – the author with much less gear only required one

Low water on the Dead River meant that the author was forced to walk much of the time. This was the same river that was at flood stage in 1775 after a hurricane

Portaging across the Canadian border and the height of land. Arnold's men left most of their bateaux behind and marched from here; the author carried his canoe across and continued via water to Quebec City

Yellow booms criss-crossed much of the upper Chaudiere as part of clean-up efforts following the massive explosion in the town of Lac Megantic – a 21st century challenge that Arnold and his men avoided

Low water again on the Chaudiere River. Arnold's men were marching along shore here but Arnold, Morgan, and a few others remained in bateaux and canoes

Grand Falls. Arnold narrowly missed a disaster here but managed to portage around, something the author certainly imitated 238 years later

Etchemin Falls. By this time all of the army was afoot so they were not forced to navigate around this feature. The author was forced to lower his canoe nearly vertically down a steep cliff face to avoid it on his journey

Looking out over the Saint Lawrence River from the mouth of the Etchemin River. Nearly there!

The first view of the Saint Lawrence River as one turns the final bend of the Etchemin River – a bittersweet experience for the author. What might Arnold have felt upon sighting a similar scene?

A profile engraving of Benedict Arnold. It was made by H. B. Hall based upon a portrait of Arnold painted by John Trumbull in 1894.

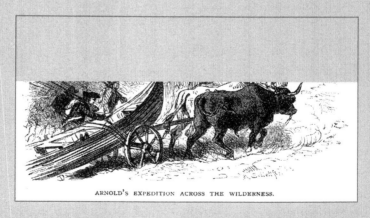

ARNOLD'S EXPEDITION ACROSS THE WILDERNESS.

An engraving of the army on the march. Note the oxen pulling the bateau-laden cart, indicative that this image depicts a portage early on in the expedition, likely before Norridgewock Falls. Civilization was left behind at the falls and the last ox was slaughtered at the Great Carrying Place.

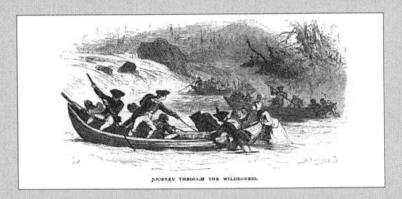

The bateaux struggling upstream. Note the myriad ways that Arnold's men (and the author centuries later) were forced to use to make progress against the current: poling, paddling, and lugging. Note also the woman clad in white pushing behind the bateau in the forground. Any women on the expedition would have had to lend a hand in the grueling work.

Portaging around Skowhegan Falls. One of the most challenging portages of the expedition, it must have gone remarkably smoothly for only a few of the journalists commented upon the obstacle. Note the nearly vertical walls that the men are hauling the bateaux up – in 2013 the author was forced to go around these cliffs due to some modern fencing. Even had he had a clear path, the route would perhaps have been insurmountable.

The army on the portage trail. This painting by N. C. Wyeth, done in 1937, likely depicts either one of the Great Carrying Place portages or the Height of Land portage. Note the snow and ice on the ground. Close examination reveals their gaunt yet determined countenances.

Mural of Attack on Quebec Expedition. After crossing the Height of Land, the expedition was mostly on foot. Here, one of the few remaining boats navigates some rapids on its way downstream.

Death of General Montgomery in the Attack on Quebec by John Trumbull, 1786. Leading one of the two flanking movements to assault Lower Town, Quebec City on New Year's Eve 1775 (Benedict Arnold led the other), General Richard Montgomery was killed after exhorting his men onwards. In the ensuing confusion, his force retreated, as did Arnold's later in the fight.

Interlude: What Did They Do For Fun?

"Our cheerfulness and hilarity still accompanied us. Incidents were perpetually occurring which furnished us with mirth and jocularity..."[1] – George Morison

One is hard pressed to visualize 1100 men trekking through the wilderness without wondering, just what did they do for fun around the campfire each night? Did they tell tall tales, play games or cards? Or were they simply too exhausted to do much besides roll up in their blankets and fall asleep? One suspects that no matter how hard the labor was during the day, the men needed a little bit of entertainment in the evenings, if for nothing else than to leaven the increasingly dark mood. And, of course, a close reading of the journals reveals a definite proclivity for jokes, games, and hilarity wherever they could be found.

George Morison wrote about some of the hijinks that took place, comparing their goofing to a comic play. "The lovers of the drama too, could they have witnessed our performances and fancied a wilderness for a theatre, might have had a plentiful entertainment, both of the tragic and comic exhibited, not by proxy, but in real life; for such indeed were our performances these three days past."[2] Occasionally it did take the form of a more organized performance. John Henry remembers that to keep their spirits up, one soldier would serenade the group. "At night, warming our bodies at an immense fire, (our compatriots joined promiscuously around,) to animate the company he would sing "Plato;" his sonorous voice gave spirit to my heart."[3] By play-acting and singing the men were able to keep morale up in a tough situation.

Frequently entertainment took a more informal form around the campfire, however. "Getchel, beside his sheer wisdom, possessed a large fund of knowledge...and much humorous anecdote, with which, in spite of our privations, he made us laugh,"[4] remembers one soldier, and no doubt story-telling made up the bulk of entertainment each evening. One can easily picture shadows flickering across the soldiers' faces as they listened to tall tale after tall tale – remember Arnold's grossly exaggerated claim to eight or ten dozen of fish caught in an hour. Storytelling was a valuable skill in the days before electronic media and able orators were widely admired. Sometimes the men had little choice but to entertain themselves throughout the evening hours. "Our encampments these two last nights were almost insupportable; for the ground was so soaked with rain that the driest situation we could find was too wet to lay upon any length of time; so that we got but little rest...we amused ourselves around our fires most all the night,"[5] wrote another during the rains along the Great Carrying Place. If they couldn't sleep, they might as well tell stories.

Among soldiers, rough-housing of course would have been frequent. Two soldiers began to fight and Simon Fobes recorded what happened next. "[Captain Hubbard] parted [the two combatants], and while endeavoring to effect a reconciliation one of them, being in a great rage, clinched him. The Captain laid the fellow down carefully by the side of a log, and held him there until he begged his pardon and promised reformation. Captain Hubbard being a large man, and good natured as he was stout, came in laughing and told what he had done."[6] These episodes and others allowed men to get out any energy and aggression remaining after the day's work.

Comicality also occurred throughout the days' work and travel as well. As the men trudged over portages and forced their way up swollen streams, they frequently found humorous circumstances, often at the expense of others. As Henry portaged to Bog Brook and the Dead River, he wrote "down we would come, waist deep in a bed of moss; such incidents always created a laugh."[7] Dearborn agreed, writing, "in Crossing a Small River on a Logg I slipt off and fell flat on my Back in the river..."[8] One can picture him chuckling to himself and shaking his head ruefully as he wrote "flat on my back..." that night. Later at camp the night after another such incident, Henry was drying his clothes by hand. "During this time, my breeches were in my hand almost in continued friction. The laugh of the company was against me but it was borne stoically."[9] Undoubtedly the story of Henry's dampening became more and more exaggerated in the retelling around dinner that evening.

Their journals also became outlets for the men to reflect humorously about the day's events, creating some excellent reading for the armchair adventurer. Henry flipped his bateau on the North Branch of the Dead River and narrated what happened next. "The art of swimming was tried, in which I thought myself adept, but it was a topsy-turvy business; the force of the water threw me often heels over head."[10] One can't help but smile at his description of the events. No doubt he too grinned as he wrote it – thankful to be alive and able to laugh about it afterwards.

Morison does an admirable job of describing how the men kept their spirits up in spite of the tough going. "We were often half leg deep in the mud, stumbling over old fallen logs, one leg sinking deeper in the mire than the other, then down goes the boat and the carriers with it." Anybody who has slogged through mud has certainly been in a similar situation and can picture the response from Morison's comrades. "A hearty laugh prevails...their comrades tauntingly asking them how they liked their washing and lodging." Yet inevitably, the reverse happens. "Perhaps a few paces further down they go, the laugh reverts upon them [and] the others, who had just before met with a like misfortune, call out to them to come here and they would go lift them." As long as everybody had thick enough skin to enjoy the good-natured badinage it worked as a salve for their troubles and hard days. Morison relates that even the most dour individual "could not have evaded a smile" given the circumstances, and he likely was correct.[11]

Yet as the expedition continued and the situation became direr, it became tougher for the men to keep their chins up. A note of sarcasm and a darker humor begins to creep into their diaries. Where Thayer might have before laughed off a fall, he now wrote, "I accidentally slipped and fell on the broad of my back, on which occasion I suffered exceedingly, having my clothes frozen to my back."[12] As the consequences of a wetting became more serious, the humor of the accidents evaporated. And monotonous hardships, day-in, day-out, dragged on even the most optimistic of spirits. "We were obliged to wade almost the whole way. Now we are learning to be soldiers,"[13] wrote Caleb Haskell bleakly. Clearly he had his limits.

Once rations ran out, the men presumably were hard-pressed to find the humorous side of anything, but still appear to have managed to find lighter moments. Henry describes the method for distributing a small amount of food among a large group of men. "Some of you have been taught how this is done: if you have forgotten, it will be well now to tell you of it. The principal of the party, if he is a gentleman and man of honor, divides the whole portion equally into as many parts as there are men, including himself; this is done under the eyes of all concerned, and with their approbation; the officer then directs some one of the company to turn his back upon him, and laying his hand on a particular portion, asks, "whose shall be this?" The answer is haphazard, A. B. &c. or any other of the party. It has frequently occurred that we were compelled to divide the necessaries of life in this way."[14] This method is a frequent resort for food distribution in survival situations and has been used by Ernest Shackleton of Endurance reknown, William Bligh of "Mutiny on The Bounty" fame, and many others. It is resorted to only under drastic circumstances but here too they found laughter. Later in the trip, dividing a small duck among ten people, "the lottery gave [Henry] victory over my respectable friend Cunningham. His share was the head and the feet, mine one of the thighs. Hungry and miserable as we were, even this was sport to us."[15] As Henry enjoyed his comparatively sumptuous portion, the men chuckled over Cunningham's bad luck.

As one soldier wrote, "Men of true spirit will beard death in every shape, even, at times, with laughter."[16] On the same day that Henry wrote about one soldier singing he described the attempts at a meal for the night. "[Moccasins] were brought to the kettle and boiled a considerable time, under the vague, but *consolatory hope that a mucilage would take place,"*[17] *without luck. That the men were able to sing and laugh in the face of starvation is testament to their indomitable spirit. In spite of their terrible situation the men were able to keep their morale up with singing, play-acting, story-telling and joking. Without a spirit of fun to keep their hopes alive, they may not have lived to tell the tale.*

Chapter 8: The Height of Land

"[The portage was] intersected with a considerable ridge covered with fallen trees, stones and brush. The ground adjacent to this ridge is swampy, plentifully strewed with old dead logs, and with every thing that could render it impassable."[1] – George Morison

Crossing the border into Canada was an exciting part of the trip for me. Because the boundary between the United States and Canada follows the height of land here, all waters in Canada drain north to the St. Lawrence and all waters in the United States drain south straight into the Atlantic. Therefore, it is inescapable that one must portage across the border. From Arnold Pond to Arnold River is approximately four miles and is one of the shorter and easier height of land portages possible. But that doesn't mean that in the 21st century a whole lot of people take advantage of this fact and I was looking forward to the faces of the border guards as I portaged up to their gate with a canoe on my shoulders and pack on my back.

    I had camped on Arnold Pond the night before so this morning I woke and paddled across Arnold Pond. The mist was just rising off the surface of the water and I paddled through the eerie half-light created by the sun's attempts to break through the fog. Morning paddles are some of my favorite and the atmosphere of this one energized me even more for the portage to come. I took out on the far side on a gravel camp road, and walked briefly to the end of it before turning left onto Rte. 27. It would take me through the Coburn Gore border patrol station into Canada.

    This was one of two circumstances where I substantially differed in my trip from the route that Arnold took in 1775. For Arnold did not go through Coburn Gore – the pass between Black Mountain to the south and Pepin Mountain to the north that the road now follows. He went through the next pass north, with Pepin Mountain now to the south on his left and Louise Mountain on his right. In 1775, with no roads and only a wilderness around, this was the easier option. Coburn Gore is a lower pass but in 1775 it was clogged with dense vegetation and rough terrain. The pass he chose offered a much simpler route, although it is slightly higher in elevation.

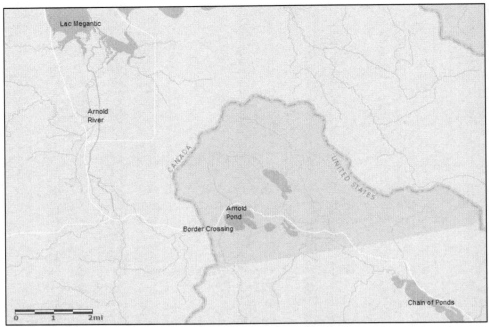

The height of land and border crossing

So in 2013, I was faced with a choice. Either trace Arnold's route exactly and bushwhack for 4 miles across the Canadian border, perhaps getting arrested in the process, or follow a nicely paved road and international law by entering Canada through Coburn Gore. Since I left Arnold Pond from the same spot he did and entered Arnold River just upstream of where he did, it would not result in any difference in the paddling between our two trips. The reader can certainly guess which option I chose – striving for exact historical accuracy was just not worth a night in a Quebec jail. So as I set off down Rte. 27, I knew I would be briefly stepping off Arnold's route. But I wasn't worried about it. If there had been a road there in 1775, he would have done the same thing.

· · ·

Just like they were for much of the trip, the army was spread out as they arrived at the Height of Land. A small party dispatched from the Great Carrying Place crossed first, surveying, blazing and clearing the route. Captain Hanchett and the advance group of fifty men arrived next, attempting to get to the settlements for relief. Arnold crossed it soon afterwards, hurrying to catch up. Knowing the paucity of provisions remaining and observing the roughness of the portage around him, he sent back a man with a note. "I think the whole will get forward much sooner by leaving all the batteaux. If there are any people sick you will perhaps be under a necessity of bringing on some batteaux."[2] Later, after navigating Arnold River (called Seven Mile Stream in the journals – it of course hadn't been named for Arnold yet) and conversing with Hanchett who had attempted to follow the stream on foot and become lost in some swamps, Arnold sent back another message to the main divisions giving clear directions to avoid those same swamps by heading east to higher ground. As we shall see later, this note would have serious consequences.

    Following the relief parties and advance scouting and clearing parties came the main body of the army, or what remained of it following Enos' defection. Morgan, Meigs, and Greene all brought their men up the North Branch of the Dead River, through the Chain of Ponds, and to Arnold Pond from which they would begin the Height of Land portage. As condition worsened and food diminished, morale began to drop. However, the men were resigned to moving forward as evinced by Henry Dearborn. "But being now almost out of Provisions we were Sure to die if we attempted to Return Back. – and We Could be in no Worse Situation if we proceeded on our rout..."[3] It was a ragtag army which emerged onto Arnold Pond but it still was an army and it was here that Arnold's first note reached many of the men, and here that we will follow the main body of the army across the Height of Land.

    The men received Arnold's order to abandon the bateaux with great happiness. "We received orders here to Leave our Batteaus, and all march by Land, We here Divided our Provisions and gave every man his part,"[4] relates Dearborn matter-of-factly. George Morison does a better job of conveying the attendant pleasure that the order must have brought when he wrote that "with inexpressible joy we dropt those grievous burthens"[5] Most companies did carry one bateau across to facilitate transportation of the sick and any heavier supplies.

    Daniel Morgan's company, however, carried seven bateaux across the Height of Land. Ignoring Arnold's orders, Morgan must have thought that they would be needed later on. He was carrying a larger part of the army's military stores at this point so he may have wanted them to continue to transport the heavy arms and ammunition. It became a trial for his men, however, and John Henry looked on in sympathy. "It would have made your heart ache to view the intolerable labors of his fine fellows. Some of them, it was said, had the flesh worn from their shoulders, even to the bone."[6] Henry censured Morgan for his strict discipline but time would demonstrate that his decision was a smart one.

    The rest of the men took what they could carry, some fabricating rustic knapsacks out of canvas cloth or wool blankets. "What little we had to carry we put into our knapsacks,"[7] wrote Abner Stocking, and Senter concurred. "Our provisions were now a very inconsiderable part of our burthen,"[8] he noted sardonically. Experimentation with non-foodstuffs as food continued, the men boiling or roasting bits of leather to eat. Simeon Thayer provides a description of the preparation: "Taking up some raw-hides, that lay for several Days in the bottom of their boats...chopping them them to pieces, singeing first the hair, afterwards boiling them and living on the juice or liquid that they soak'd from it for a considerable time."[9] The following day he did manage to kill a partridge and others still found fish but one soldier summed it up for the vast majority of the men when he wrote that they were, "as hungry as wolves, and nothing to eat."[10] Relief couldn't arrive fast enough.

By this time few of the men were able to enjoy their surroundings. At the height of land with tall mountains all around, it must have been an inspiring sight and Henry wrote when he passed through with the scouting party earlier that "It made an impression upon us that was really more chilling than the air which surrounded us."[11] But by now the army was only able to focus on one thing: making progress towards relief. A storm passed through as they neared the Height of Land and "the day was very cold and the ground covered in pretty deep snow which had fell in the night." They "forced a passage, the most difficult of any we had yet performed. The ascent and descent of the hill was inconceivably difficult...this day's movement was by far the most oppressive of any we had experienced." George Morison summed it up when he wrote that "we denominated [it] the Terrible Carrying Place; a dismal portage indeed."[12] It was yet another trial for the army to endure. But endure they did and kept moving forward.

. . .

Posted road signs were my first warning that I was nearing the checkpoint to cross into Canada. I finally rounded the last corner and saw the lights and gate in front of me. With the canoe on my shoulders and pack on my back, I walked right up to the gate as a flurry of activity occurred inside the checkpoint. A man stepped out quickly and took one good look at me before yelling back over his shoulder, "Marquez canoe! Marquez canoe!" gleefully. He of course wanted whoever was inside to write "canoe" into the blank spot for "Vehicle Type," and clearly couldn't have been more pleased with his own wit. He walked over to me grinning.

"Good morning! How are you doing?" I told him I was heading to Quebec, which seemed to impress him. He proceeded to ask all the standard questions about fresh fruit and vegetables, length of stay, and everything else they seem to want to know about.

"Do you have any weapons?"

"Just an axe and a pocket-knife," I answered. He didn't seem to be too worried. "Yes, yes. To chop firewood. I understand," he responded and moved on to the next one, where my answer gave him pause.

"How much money do you have?"

"Oh I've got about fifty dollars," I replied, speaking for the cash currently in my wallet.

He looked aghast. "I can't let you in! I'm sorry but that is not..."

I cut him off. "I have more in the bank! Lots in the bank and a credit card with me." His relief was palpable – he truly thought he might have to stop me from entering Quebec.

He performed a cursory search of my gear, sped up no doubt by the smell that was beginning to permeate all my clothing. In spite of that shower in Stratton, nine days of camping had left me a little rank. He wished me luck, then asked what river I was taking to get down to Quebec.

To my answer "The Chaudière," he began to look worried again. "Be very careful. I don't know anybody who has paddled that before. There are lots of rapids and rocks. Be careful," he reiterated and then, with a disbelieving shake of his head, wished me well. I packed up my gear, shouldered the load, and walked off. I was in Canada! No doubt Arnold felt much more poignantly about the achievement than I did but it was still a milestone and I was pleased to be there.

It was nearly three more miles to the put-in on the Arnold River. It was also, however, primarily downhill and I was making good time along the road edge as cars and trucks whizzed by. Many tooted their horns to say hello and I waved to each in recognition of their support. Then one small blue car whizzed by, pulled over into the gravel margin, turned around, and came back before parking next to me. "Uh-oh," I thought. "What have I done now? I don't think I'm trespassing!"

A short, slim, middle-aged man with glasses and a mustache stepped out. I stopped as he approached and in halting English he asked if I was following Arnold's route. I won't be able to recreate here the paucity of his knowledge of the English language but he managed to convey that he was a reporter for the local newspaper and he wanted to interview me.

Between his bad English and my worse French, we managed to hold one. He asked about the trip to-date, the hardest part, the prettiest part, and all the basic interview questions a non-paddler might think of. When we finished, he promised that it would be in the next edition of his paper, which I understood to be based out of the town of Lac Megantic. With many thanks, he took a couple pictures and then climbed back into his car and left. Later, after the trip, I found his article online. He had got most of the information correct and I was pleased to find out that little had been lost in translation.

The road finally mellowed out as it came out of the hills and mountains along the border. I passed several houses and then a farm or two as I neared Arnold River. These farms were perhaps taking advantage of a quirk of ecology that Arnold's men noticed in 1775. As they neared the end of their Height of Land portage, they inexplicably came upon a large meadow nestled in amongst the thick trees and brush of the Canadian woods. They promptly named it "Beautiful Meadow" and it was here that the next scene in their drama took place.

. . .

"Beautiful Meadow" must have seemed to be a gift sent from heaven. Many of the journalists mention it and all saw it as a respite from their travails. Arnold and Hanchett with their small groups of men were still out front but the remainder of the army met up here, the lead elements camping in the meadow to allow the rear guard to catch up.

Among other things, this allowed Enos' defection to now become common knowledge (although Arnold himself, being out in front, still was unaware). Dearborn summed up the general sentiment of the men when he wrote that, "Our men made a General Prayer, that Colo: Enos and all his men, might die by the way, or meet with some disaster."[13] Their turning back had a dual effect: one of uniting the remaining men in their anger at Enos' cowardliness to continue to march onwards in spite of Enos' decision, but also a second one of permitting a sneaking suspicion that perhaps Enos has made the right decision. After all, they weren't out of the woods yet.

With only one bateau per company now, the men had relegated themselves to a minimalist approach to marching. Carrying only what little food they still had, their rifles and a little ammunition, and not much else, they were sleeping in the open and roughing it. With snow continuing to fall, this could not have been comfortable, but it was the best they could do in the situation.

Taking the opportunity that having the army together permitted, the men combined all remaining food and then split it up evenly among everybody present. Given that some soldiers, at least according to their journals, had gone without rationed sustenance for several days now, the resulting allotments are a little surprising. Some companies must have still been carrying a barrel or two of flour for each man received "5 pints of flour and 2 oz. of meat."[14] Since 600 men remained on the expedition (minus approximately 60 men who were with either Arnold or Hanchett), this meant that the expedition had just over 1000 pounds of flour to disperse. Among 540 men, that is not a lot. Pork, the meat in question, was nearly used up and the officers in a real display of leadership and sympathy for their men, "were in general generous enough to dispense with [the pork] for the better satisfaction and encouragement of the soldiers."[15]

There remained a general presentiment that "Col. Enos… had returned with three companies, and taken large stores of provisions,"[16] though whether or not he actually returned with extra rations we may never know. Regardless, the men would be forced to make do with what they had left, and what they could scavenge. Senter references fish caught in the Arnold River, and Thayer managed to catch a partridge nearby, but these were mere mouthfuls. The men were too focused on simply getting to the settlements and relief to take the necessary time to hunt, and even if they had there is no reason to suspect that they might have been successful.

Upon the division of the remaining food, four companies immediately set off downstream, tracing Seven Mile Stream (present-day Arnold River) towards Lac Megantic. They wanted to make some ground while there was still daylight. The rest of the army tarried at Beautiful Meadow for the evening, including Morgan's men who were perhaps the most exhausted having carried their bateaux across the Height of Land portage in less than a day. While resting and attempting to regain their strength in the meadow, some men decided to let fate take over at this point. In the words of Dr. Senter, "several of the men devoured the whole of their flour the last evening, determined (as they expressed it,) to have a full meal, letting the morrow look out for itself."[17] They would rue this decision.

These men opted for such a course perhaps after receiving a letter from Arnold, delivered by a messenger who arrived at Beautiful Meadow sometime the afternoon of October 28th. He somehow missed four companies who had already departed from the rendez-vous, but was able to deliver Arnold's communique to the remainder still camping at the meadow.

It included a variety of uplifting information, not all of it strictly true. Most heartening for the men, Arnold wrote that, "I hope to be [at the French settlements] in three days," and will "send back provisions as soon as possible." This was promptly repeated and embellished to be that "provisions will arrive in three days", perhaps leading to the impetuous decision of some to eat all their rations at once. Arnold also wrote that definite word had been received of the disposition of the French inhabitants, and that they "are rejoiced to hear we are coming, and that they will gladly supply us with provisions."[18] To add to the good news, only a few soldiers were reported to be stationed at Quebec.

All this positive news must have lightened the tired and hungry men's spirits considerably. Furthermore, as a post script, Arnold wrote specific directions for moving forward towards the Chaudière River. Instead of following Arnold River (as the four impatient companies who had already departed had done), "strike off to the right hand and keep about a north and by east course, which will escape the low swampy land and save a very great distance."[19] This would have worked except that Arnold's map was incorrect. Two bodies of water, Rush Lake and Spider Lake, blocked this way and would create an obstacle which would nearly destroy the expedition when it was at its weakest.

. . .

The farm along the Arnold River that I put in next to bore no sign of meeting at Beautiful Meadow that occurred 240 years ago (although a sign nearby pointed towards the "Arnold Motel"). A man nearby repaired a guardrail as cars whizzed past. Life in the 21st century continued.

I left my canoe at the riverside, thankful to be free of the load, and walked a little bit further down the road, half-heartedly searching for a hot meal. After a couple hundred yards and no sign of an approaching town, however, I gave up and turned around. I had plenty of food with me and could get something in the town of Lac Megantic on the north end of the lake by the same name.

From here on out, my water route would be tracing only a small fraction of the army. Since most companies had left nearly all their bateaux on the other side of the portage, I would be following by canoe an army primarily marching on the land abutting the river. However, Arnold, Morgan and his company, and a few other small groups of men continued on the river. I was content that this remained the best way to travel the route. Besides, walking on what is now a paved road is no way to embrace history. So I loaded my gear into my boat and set off down the Arnold River, avoiding the heap of trouble that the army would get into by trying to walk along the shore. But that, as they say, is a story for the next chapter.

Interlude: The Women of Arnold's Army

"My mind was humbled yet astonished at the exertions of this good woman."[1] – John Henry

Eighteenth century armies were really two armies in one: the soldiers and their officers, armaments, equipment, and baggage only composed one half of the mass of moving people that was known as an army. The second was often as large and was composed of camp followers – the wives and children of the soldiers themselves, along with others trying to make a living off the army like itinerant peddlers and prostitutes. As was noted in a previous Interlude, the wives of the men serving played an important role in the army – helping to cook, mend clothes, wash, and even nurse sick or injured men. They might even be paid – either in an official capacity or simply on the side by an individual man. They were an accepted institution, and were an integral part of most Revolutionary War armies as well.

However, due to the anticipated hardships of Arnold's march (understated as they had been at the beginning), historians know of only four women who left Cambridge with Benedict Arnold's army. Of those, we can only be sure that two of them reached Quebec – the other two may have turned back at some point early in the expedition or perhaps with Enos when his division returned. The two successful women were Jemima Warner, wife of James Warner, and Suzannah Grier, the wife of Sergeant Joseph Grier. Yet in spite of the fact that only two women are known by name to posterity, the journalists gave us some surprisingly telling anecdotes of these women's participation in the expedition.[2]

Before we look at these two women, a quick peek at other mentionings of women is in order. Abner Stocking made the first mention, back in Newburyport, when he wrote that "many pretty Girls stood upon the shore, I suppose weeping for the departure of their sweethearts."[3] Indeed, most did stay home – the expedition was no place for the light of heart, man or woman.

Because of this, many men pined after their wives or girlfriends throughout the expedition, and those with women at home to write to did, frequently. Return Meigs' journal is peppered with references to his wife. "I wrote this day to my honored father and to Mrs. Meigs," he noted one day. Five days later, "I wrote...two letters to Mrs. Meigs," and soon after, "This day I wrote to Mrs. Meigs."[4] He clearly missed her – the company of men in the wilderness certainly did not supplant her. Somewhere perhaps a repository of these letters still exists. If it does, it will be a treasure trove for the Arnold scholar.

Major Timothy Bigelow was also a prolific letter writer, and we have access to a few he wrote his wife, Anna. On October 26th, worried about the worsening food situation and what might lie ahead, he penned, "We are in a wilderness nearly one hundred miles from any inhabitants...and but about five days provisions...If the French are our enemies it will go hard with us, for we have no retreat left. In that case there will be no alternative between the sword and famine." He ended his letter on a bitter note, afraid he might never see her again. "May God in his infinite mercy protect you, my more than ever dear wife, and my dear children, Adieu, and ever believe me to be your most affectionate husband."[5] Fortunately for both of them, he made it out of the woods. The letter's final sentence would have been a rather morbid note to end on, had it been his last communication. His next note was much more uplifting. "I very much regret my writing the last letter to you, the contents were so gloomy...We have had a very fatiguing march of it, but I hope it will soon be over."[6] He too relished the thought of returning to his wife.

Both Meigs and Bigelow as well as many others must have frequently looked with envy at Sergeant Joseph Grier and Private James Warner who had their wives by their side. These women, however, were forced to struggle alongside the men, enduring all the same privations and adversity that the rest of the army did. It caused some journalists no end of admiration. "Mrs. Grier has got before me," wrote Henry while trudging through the swamps surrounding Arnold River. "Her clothes more than waist high, she waded before me to firm ground. No one, so long as she was known to us, dared to intimate a disrespectful idea of her." She kept up with her husband and endured the hardships stoically with all the others. "My mind was humbled, yet astonished, at the exertions of this good woman,"[7] he summed up, clearly awestruck.

Jemima Warner, if possible, inspired even more reverence than Mrs. Grier. Henry described James Warner as, "a man who lagged on every occasion." Again lost in the swamps near Arnold River and Lac Megantic, Warner became separated from the company. "He had sat down, sick, under a tree, a few miles back," someone remembered. Clearly distraught, "his wife begged us to wait a short time, and with tears of affection in her eyes, ran back to her husband."[8] Abner Stocking picks up the tale from there. "His affectionate wife tarryed by him until he died, while the rest of the company proceeded on their way. Having no implements with which she could bury him she covered him with leaves, and then took his gun and other implements and left him with a heavy heart." This caring woman, dedicated to her husband, returned to his side alone while the army pushed on. Once he had died, with nothing left to do, she picked up his gun and marched onwards. Amazed, Stocking wrote, "after travelling 20 miles she came up with us."[9] Her strength of body and character must have stirred the men to greater heights.

When the expedition finally reached civilization on the French side, the men understandably gravitated towards food first. Liquor came next for some but one of the other benefits of civilization was the reappearance of women in their lives. Moses Kimball gives us a sense of his priorities in a journal entry for November 5th. "Went 6 miles & stop'd at a clever old Frenchman's house where they gave us rum & bread & butter, as much as we wanted. There was two pretty girls at the same house." His next line for the same day is eloquent for its implications. "Stayed till the next day."[10] A house with rum, food, and pretty girls was not to be passed up lightly. Several other soldiers recorded similar instances of meeting beautiful women and dallying in their company. Even with the imminent siege in the future, the men had missed female company too much to breeze past.

Unhappily, the stories of Suzannah Grier and Jemima Warner did not end well. Both these women made it to Quebec City, Suzannah Grier still in the company of her husband and Jemima Warner now alone. Soon after the siege of Quebec began, Jemima Warner was "killed by a shot from the city [likely an artillery round]."[11] In April, long after the desperate New Year's Eve attack on the city and far into the drawn out stalemate between sides, Caleb Haskell also recorded the death of Suzannah Grier. "A woman belonging to the Pennsylvania troops was killed to-day by accident – a soldier carelessly snapping his musket which proved to be loaded."[12] Like so many of the men who made the march, the expedition ultimately proved fatal for these women as well. But the anecdotes passed down regarding their intrepid deeds during the march stand as a testament to their enduring strength and fortitude.

Chapter 9: The Arnold River and Lac Megantic

"We proceeded with as little knowledge of where we were, or where we should get to, as if we had been in the unknown interior of Africa, or the deserts of Arabia."[1] – Dr. Isaac Senter

The Arnold River is a fast-flowing river that has many of the characteristics of a mountains stream. It was only inches deep where I put in but, due to its speed, I was able to bump and grind my way through. Large, rounded and white boulders dotted the stream, contrasting sharply with the murky brown of the water. Definitely an agricultural river with significant run-off problems, I could smell the effluvia of the water for much of its length.

But the speed with which I descended offset all that. Downstream at last! It felt good to be traveling so fast. But there was little time to celebrate – the boniness of the river necessitated a quick eye and quicker paddle and I was kept busy on both sides of the canoe navigating between obstructions. Farmland whipped by me as I dodged one rock after another.

Soon, however, the stream began to flatten out. As it left the foothills of the divide over which I had just portaged it began to take on a calmer appearance and partake of the occasional meander. Instead of grown trees denoting a thin littoral zone between river and farm, cultivated areas began to give way to brushier lowlands and trees began to shorten and then disappear altogether. I was entering the swamps of Arnold River, the place that would give the army one of its final endurance tests and ultimately cost the lives of dozens.

. . .

If the reader recalls, Arnold and Hanchett had descended the Arnold River first (and separately): Arnold by bateaux and Hanchett on foot. They were striking into unknown territory – no scouts had made it to the Arnold River (John Henry and his scouting party had climbed a tree just past the divide for a long view but had travelled no further) and no messengers from the settlements had returned. So they were moving forward blindly.

Arnold reached Lac Megantic with little trouble. By traveling in his bateaux he was able to make good time, although, as he described, the river "is

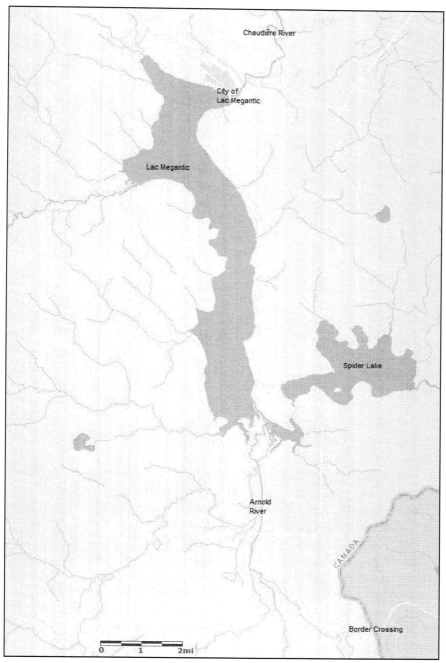
The Arnold River and Lac Megantic

very crooked & runs to all points of the Compass: we met many obstructions of Loggs, &c. which we were obliged to cut away."[2] Partway down he met his messenger that had been sent ahead to the settlements. It was with this news that he would send one Isaac Hull back to the army, telling of the nearness of relief, the friendly disposition of the inhabitants, and the minimal fortifications at Quebec. Arnold continued on and paddled across the southern end of Lac Megantic as the sun was setting to a bark hut on the eastern shore, to await Hanchett's men who were proceeding by land.

Hanchett did not have the easy time of it that Arnold did. Keeping to the eastern shore of Arnold River, he and his men "waded through two miles thro' water to their waists." They bogged down in the swamps abutting the river, the very ones that were whipping by me in 2013. And once they reached the lake, they were stuck. With no boats they could go no further, so they shouted desperately for aid. Soaking wet in near freezing temperatures, they were in real need of help. Luckily, Arnold heard their yells and "discovered them on a Point of low Land" and "immediately sent all the Battoes for them." After several ferries, they were reunited on Lac Megantic, ready to proceed towards the French settlements on the Chaudière River.

With Hanchett's experience in mind, Arnold also directed Hull to inform the army to "by no means keep the brook," but "strike off to the right hand and keep about a north by east course, which will escape the low swampy land"[3] that Hanchett had just waded through. Hull set out the following morning towards the main body of the army where we'll catch up with him in a minute.

The only problem with these directions was that two large bodies of water blocked anyone from following Arnold's instructions: Rush Lake and Spider Lake. Arnold must have had no knowledge of them to write such patently false instructions to his men. But how did he not know of their existence?

Historian Justin Smith provides the answer. Anyone navigating the Arnold River today emerges from the river onto a broad stream leaving Rush Lake for Lac Megantic. If Arnold had traveled the river today, he could not have missed Rush Lake – it is visible from the junction. But in 1775, the Arnold River had a very different route. A clogged deadwater called the Black Arnold, impassable today and barely noticeable, held the main current of the river. Instead of an outlet on Rush River, it poured directly into Lac Megantic further west. No visual of Rush Lake is provided. Montresor in 1761 had traveled Arnold River in the dark and Arnold himself arrived at Lac Megantic at dusk. The outlet from Rush Lake was unknown to Montresor who left it unmarked on his maps or in his journal and Arnold had no reason to suspect either Rush or Spider Lake's existence, nor might he have seen it in the fading twilight. Assuming only land existed there and knowing Hanchett's travails wading through the swamps, he ordered his army to the presumed high land. It was a mistake that would cost them.[4]

Hull, traveling back upstream (presumably by canoe to avoid the swamps), somehow missed the anxious companies of Dearborn, Goodrich, Ward and Smith. Remember these four companies had set off from "Beautiful Meadow" before Hull – Arnold's messenger – returned. The missed connection here meant that these four companies entered the same swamps around Arnold River that Hanchett had just waded through. Goodrich, searching for a passage, "was almost perished with the Cold, having Waded Several Miles Backwards, and forwards, Sometimes to his Arm-pits in Water & Ice, endeavouring to find some place to Cross this River."[5] While Goodrich and Dearborn managed to get out with the help of another canoe, darkness caught up to the rest who were forced to spend the night in the swamps.

It only compounded their wretchedness. On a small piece of high ground – likely one of the few around, the men set up camp. "We got on a little knoll of land...where we were obliged to stay, night coming on, and we were all cold and wet; one man fainted in the water with fatigue and cold, but was helped along," writes James Melvin, who takes up the narrative. He described the measures they went to to start a fire. "We had to wade into the water, and chop down trees, fetch the wood out of the water after dark to make a fire to dry ourselves." It must have been a night with little sleep. "The water surrounding us close to our heads; if it had rained hard it would have overflown the place we were in."[6] Exhaustion, hunger, cold, and wet were all combining to exacerbate the fear the men were beginning to feel crawl around in their guts. "Would they make it out alive?" must have been in the forefront of their minds for most of their waking hours. At this point, it was hard to say.

The following morning Dearborn and Goodrich, with their canoe and one bateau shuffled their men slowly out of the swamps and across the mouths of the Dead Arnold (a branch of the main river at the outlet) and Rush Rivers. "Geting a Cross these Two rivers took up the Chief of the day," wrote Dearborn, but "Before Sun Set we all arrived at the Bark-House Safe," - the same bark hut Arnold had used. The men thankfully rested here before continuing along the shore of Megantic to the mouth of the Chaudière River. Arnold, Hanchett, and Morgan (he had carried his bateaux across the Height of Land and descended the Arnold River easily via water) were all in front. Greene's division and two other companies were behind them, taking supposed advantage of Arnold's directions to keep to the high ground but in reality getting into an even worse mess than anyone else did.

· · ·

The remainder of the Arnold River for myself was a pleasant paddle. I twisted in and out of oxbows as the river seemed to curl back in upon itself. Alders and other low bushes reached out from the river banks and draped their branches over the water, sometimes trailing leaves in the current. Gray clouds overhead began to give way to sunshine. Birds flitted in and out of the brush and reeds, multi-colored and full of song.

Where Dearborn's men had camped in icy water and struggled to start a fire, I watched two individuals installing bird houses every couple hundred yards. Where they had struggled through waist deep water to cross streams, I easily glided past. Here more than anywhere else, the contrast between our two experiences was the greatest. Now that they had left their bateaux behind them, traveling became increasingly arduous. It is tough to follow a water route on foot.

Eventually I entered Lac Megantic through a morass of rotting stumps and mud. The dam at the north end kept the water high enough that it had killed some of the vegetation along the water's edge here. The prevailing winds appeared to pile up drifting debris here as well, adding to the quagmire. I escaped it quickly and with a few strokes was out on the open water.

The southern end was fairly empty of houses but as I began to make progress northwards, buildings became increasingly ubiquitous. I stopped for lunch on a spit of beach and enjoyed a sandwich with a stiff breeze blowing through my hair. By the time I reached the town of Lac Megantic the houses were cheek by jowl. And what houses they were!

When I left the United States in Maine, I had left via a typical north-country town. Eustis, Maine exists as an outpost, catering to logging primarily with the occasional outdoor tourist coming to hike or ski. While surviving, it certainly was not booming. But upon nearing Lac Megantic, it was clear that this was an area that was doing well. Million-dollar houses lined the shores, complete with gables, patios, and outbuildings. Perfectly coiffed lawns were dotted with ornamental shrubs and it appeared that the more outdoor lighting you had installed, the greater your prestige in town. Some houses were covered in lamps of all types.

To be sure, the occasional working man's house appeared, but even these had large boats parked on the lake. Each boat had its own miniature mechanized elevator and frame so that when not in use, it could be cranked up several feet out of the water. On this trip, this was certainly the first time I'd seen anything like this.

I gawked as I paddled along, snapping pictures of the houses I viewed to be the gaudiest. No one appeared outdoors but this was not too big a surprise – it was mid-day midweek. Everyone was likely at work, earning the money needed to install their next outdoor lighting fixture.

I couldn't help but think that Arnold would have been thankful had anything like this been here in 1775. While I viewed these gargantuan houses as more or less a blight upon the landscape, Arnold would have been praising them as his saving grace. Even a rustic settlement would have sufficed. But it was not to be – French settlements had not crept this far south yet in 1775 and Arnold still had miles to make before reaching the first houses. So while I was taking in the sights and sounds of Megantic after effortlessly getting down the Arnold River, the army was still hungry and many companies were still lost in the swamps far to my east, circumnavigating Rush and Spider Lakes.

. . .

We've left the army dotted across the landscape in our narrative. Arnold and Morgan made it down the Arnold River in their bateaux and canoes. Hanchett struggled through the swamp directly abutting the river before being rescued by Arnold. And four companies led by Goodrich, Dearborn, Ward and Smith struggled through the same swamps before self-rescuing using only a canoe and one bateau. That leaves the remainder of the army to follow Isaac Hull and Arnold's instructions to stay further east, away from the Arnold River and neighboring swamps.

As before noted, however, Arnold had not counted on Rush or Spider Lakes. The appearance of these bodies of water flabbergasted Hull and the men who were expecting an easy, water-free march. The swamps bordering these lakes brought no comfort either. "After walking a few hours in the swamp we seemed to have lost all sense of feeling in our feet and ankles," wrote Abner Stocking. "The top of the ground was covered with a soft moss, filled with water and ice...As we were constantly slipping, we walked in great fear of breaking our bones or dislocating our joints. But to be disenabled from walking in this situation was sure death." He looked around himself and saw only misery and barren terrain, void of any of the necessaries of life. "I thought we were probably the first human being that ever took up their residence for a night in this wilderness...for I believe no wild animals would inhabit it [either]."[7]

They soon lost faith in Hull, their guide. "The pretended pilot was not less frightened than many of the rest; added to that the severe execrations he received from the front of the army to the rear, made his office not a little disagreeable," wrote Senter. He and Greene took over, swapping back and forth a compass to navigate with. "We wandered through hideous swamps and mountainious precipices, with the conjoint addition of cold, wet and hunger, not to mention our fatigue." Morale plummeted, and "several of the men towards evening were ready to give up any thoughts of ever arriving at the desired haven."[8]

Around this same time a disturbing order given by at least some of the officers to the men, not just to this group but to the whole of the remaining army. Simeon Fobes wrote that, "The officers said we must now each take care of himself,"[9] this spoken just after the food distribution in Beautiful Meadow. Morison wrote of a similar circumstance on November 1st. "It was therefore given out this morning by our officers, for every man to shift for himself, and save his own life if possible."[10] This is a worrisome circumstance, and although anarchy did not break out, it might have with an order like this. It is demonstrative of just how far the army had sunk, and what lengths the officers felt were needed to survive.

At this point of crisis, the miraculous occurred. An American Indian, speaking English, appeared and took over as guide. He surefootedly led them the remaining distance around the lakes, sticking to higher ground to avoid the swampy perimeter. It was still rough-going but with a guide who knew what he was doing, the men followed willingly. After what must have seemed like ages, they finally came within sight of Megantic once again. There, they spotted some footprints, likely those of one of the four forward divisions, and followed them to Lac Megantic. "Our arrival here was succeeded with three huzzas," wrote an elated and exhausted Dr. Senter, "and then came to our encampment."[11] The last fraction of the army had made it past Megantic and arrived at the Chaudière River. However spent, hungry, and cold they were, they knew that all they had to do was follow the river to find relief.

. . .

As I rounded the final point on Lac Megantic - traveling by water, not land – an unexpected sight greeted me. The town of Lac Megantic, normally a bustling municipality of 6000 with an active transportation industry, was one gigantic construction site. From nearly a mile away I could see cranes arcing across the sky. The beeps, honks, and whistles of heavy machinery drifted across the water. As I drew closer, it was only confirmed – the town appeared to be renovating every single building within its boundaries.

On July 5th, 2013, just under two months before my arrival, a 74-car freight train was parked in the Nantes train depot, just west of Lac Megantic. It was left unattended overnight and early in the morning of July 6th began to roll downhill towards Lac Megantic. It derailed in the center of the town and exploded, killing dozens and incinerating many of the buildings in town. It was the worst train disaster since 1864 for Canada, and it was the clean-up and rebuilding efforts from this catastrophe that I was seeing.

As I passed the marina on shore and neared the town docks, yellow booms stretched across the entrances to these slips. These booms would become the bane of my downstream push on the Chaudière, something I was not yet aware of. They were part of the clean-up effort, an attempt to corral the tens of thousands of gallons of oil spilled into the waterways and now floating downstream on the Chaudière. Environmental clean-up efforts were in full force throughout my time on the river, and these first yellow booms were only the tip of the iceberg.

I searched for an appropriate take-out around the Lac Megantic dam, and finally coasted ashore behind a gas station. The owner was out back smoking a cigarette and since my French does not include the word for "take out" I mostly gestured to ask permission to use his stairs and back alley. He, preoccupied with his smoke break, waved in agreement. Finally, I had avoided trespassing!

I emerged from behind the convenience store with pack on my back and canoe on my shoulders, next to one of the major intersections in town. To my left was a bridge across the outlet of the lake and the beginnings of the Chaudière River. The bridge was closed – all of down-town to my left was devastated and no public traffic, automobile or otherwise, was allowed in. It was one massive construction site. To my right were the main roads leading south and east. In front of me were several police officers and myriad orange traffic cones. Chain link fences crisscrossed the terrain and the air was filled with dust and noise. Jackhammers rang in the background and Caterpillar-branded equipment trundled back and forth before me, dwarfing my own load. For a man like me who had been paddling on solitary rivers for the last couple of days, it was quite overwhelming.

I took a minute to allow my senses to adjust and then let a traffic cop wave me across the road. I dodged Jersey barriers and orange barrel cones, then followed the road north-east. I passed a bank, tire store, grocery, gym, and car dealership among other businesses, with passersby gawking. In a town with so much going on and an unprecedented recovery effort underway, I was still apparently something unique to look at. Several questions flew at me and then over my head – my French was worse than I had thought because I didn't understand a thing. I simply smiled in agreement, hoping that worked.

I finally picked a likely looking couple and stammered out, "Où est la meilleure place pour aller à la rivière?" I think I asked, "Where is the best place to go to the river?" but I could be mistaken. They seemed to understand however and pointed me in the correct direction.

I took a left onto a quieter street, thankful to escape the disbelieving stares, and followed it to the parking lot of a trucking company. Still unsure as to how to pass through the wall of businesses and homes to get to the river without climbing a fence, I happily spotted a biker emerging from a heretofore unseen gap in a chain link fence. I headed towards it and found a hidden trail down to an ATV bridge over the river.

A group of ten or twelve men and women, decked out in yellow uniforms, stood around several ATVs. Yellow booms criss-crossed the river downstream from them – I'll give some more detail on these as later I try to cross them. I set my canoe down at the water's edge with the whole group watching me in silence. Unsure if I was doing something wrong, I simply kept packing and organizing gear, waiting for someone to stop me. But no one did. They just kept silently watching.

As I climbed into my boat, I decided to leaven the air. I made a joke about the size of the fish that could be caught with the booms, pointing to them and gesturing to emphasize the proportions of the potential catch. It went over like a fart in church. The whole group stared stoically at me. Either the joke didn't translate well or I was not as funny as I thought. Or my French was just that terrible. So I hung my head, grabbed my paddle, and quickly pulled a couple of times to escape the crew. It didn't matter - I was on the Chaudière at last!

Interlude: What Kept Them Going?

"Death would have been a welcome messenger to have ended our woes."[1] – George Morison

George Morison is needlessly exaggerating when he writes that "Death would have been a welcome messenger…" As several historians have pointed out before me, he could have ended his own suffering himself at any time. He didn't. So what kept him going? What kept them all going in spite of the starvation, fatigue, cold, and wet? In spite of all the obstacles thrown in the army's path, 600 made it to Quebec. But some also turned back with Enos – what did the others have that these men did not?

If the reader will remember, the trip was composed solely of volunteers. The expedition was seen as "a grand adventure" by many and far more applied for spots on the trip than were able to go. This fact alone is an important contributor to the men's perseverance. The constant gripe of working men everywhere – "I don't want to be here, but I have to be because it's work and the boss told me to do it," no longer applies. By signing up for the trip, the men were committing to the trip, through thick and thin, and while none specifically elaborated upon this point something like, "I signed up for this, so I better see it through," must have been in the back of their minds.

And it really was seen as an adventure. "Our men are much fatigued…however their spirit and industry seems to overcome every obstacle -& they appear very cheerfull,"[2] wrote Arnold early in the trip. As any stalwart body who has participated in a long expedition, whether it is trekking or paddling or some other form of transportation, can attest, part of the joy of traveling through the wilderness is coming up against obstacles and then beating them. It is human nature to rise to challenge. Even those few faint-hearted individuals among the army must have been buoyed up at the sight of so many others rising to the occasion and conquering the Kennebec, the Great Carrying Place, and the Dead River. For every rapid, falls, storm, mishap, and complication resulted in a success story. The army surmounted all difficulties and kept making progress. When Arnold wrote to George Washington with his men at the Height of Land, he used similar words to describe the morale around him. "Our march has been attended with an amazing deal of fatigue, which the officers and men have borne with cheerfulness."[3] He was able to write this after the flood and after food supplies were becoming scarce – these were just a few more obstacles to overcome.

As the army made progress, it was not just man versus nature, each trying to succeed alone. Instead, with each passing hour the men formed closer and closer bonds with each other. They were becoming a brotherhood of men, and if someone failed, he was letting down the brotherhood. John Henry, upon returning from his scouting mission, wrote, "We now found ourselves at home in the bosom of a society of brave men, with whom we were not only willing but anxious to meet the brunts of war."[4] Should any single man fail, he was not only failing himself but all the men around him. Not many were willing to do that.

One noteworthy example of this fortitude and desire to continue was the disposition of the men who were indeed forced to return to Maine due to sickness or injury. George Morison describes the scene: "Several sunk under the weight of [fatigue]. Their strength was exhausted; grew sick; and as our provisions were vanishing away, it was deemed proper to send them back. Who could not have been touched with pity and admiration for these brave men, struggling with ruthless toil and sickness and endeavoring to conceal their situation? When any of their comrades would remark to them that the[y] would not be able to advance much farther, they would raise up their half-bent bodies and force an animated look into their ghastly countenances, observing at the same time that they would soon be well enough."[5] Men did not want to return. In spite of the back-breaking labor and unrelenting toil, they wanted to continue to fight onwards towards Quebec.

Except some did turn back. Enos, his officers, and nearly 400 men decided to quit on the Dead River and return to civilization (and a court-martial). What happened?

It's hard to say. Roger Enos himself pointed to all the hardships that the mean underwent including weather and food. But these factors affected the whole army, not just his division. As outlined above, Enos also read Arnold's order differently than Arnold had intended, and returned with his whole army since he could not provide the adequate rations for them. This too, however, was not the decision other commanding officers reached. So why did Enos turn back when others didn't?

Many historians point to poorer leadership as a likely reason. Instead of quelling dissent and worry, Enos and his officers enhanced it by participating in it themselves. Unlike Arnold's model which was to have a perennial sunny outlook on all events, the officers in the fourth division saw a bleaker future for the army. Indeed, when Enos left, it was by all accounts with a tearful goodbye for Enos' men thought that the remainder of the army pushing onwards would disappear into the wilderness.

Other possible reasons include a disconnect between his division and the rest of the army. As the rearguard he was bogged down with much of the army's provision and supplies. Moving slower than the rest, there was a certain lack of communication between his division and many of the others. Arnold's charisma and the resultant uplift among men near him was distilled by the time it reached the back. And any loafers or dawdlers would naturally have drifted back to Enos' divison, perhaps sowing additional discord as well.

Regardless of the reasons, by the time the army reached Beautiful Meadow and it became generally known that Enos had returned morale was sagging. The food situation and final distribution of rations, with a blanket of snow on the ground, combined with general fatigue and weariness meant that the men were nearing the breaking point. News from Arnold that he was nearing the settlements and would send relief soon buoyed the men but at this point only a slender straw was needed to push them over the edge into despair. The swamps around Megantic and Spider Lake were that tipping point.

The men were exhausted. "Our weakness was now so great that a small twig across the way was sufficient to bring the stoutest of us to the ground," wrote Morison soon after emerging, hyperbolizing their weakness yet aptly describing their state. "Hope was now partly extinguished; and its place supplied with a deep insensibility."[6] John Henry concurred, writing, "To me the world had lost its charms. Gladly would death have been received as an auspicious herald from the Divinity....the idea occurred, and the means were in my hands, of ending existence."[7] Morbid reflections indeed. The men had been reduced to simple automatons, marching merely because there was no alternative.

Emblematic of the loss of morale was the order that circulated soon after the rendez-vous at Beautiful Meadow. As noted above, each were ordered to "shift for himself, and save his own life if possible." Morison tries to explain it, writing "Many of the men began to fall behind and those in any condition to march were scarcely able to support themselves; so that it was impossible for us to bring them along; and if we tarried with them, we must all have perished."[8] Yet leaving men to die in the wilderness could not have been easy and must have contributed to a burgeoning sense of doom.

Another example of the loss of order and discipline is more understandable but just as regrettable. James Melvin managed to escape the swamps with his company, stashed his food, and returned to help some others. Upon returning to the food cache, he "found that our provision was stolen by Captain Morgan's company."[9] While stealing supplies from others was a time-honored aspect of Revolutionary-era army life, doing it under starvation circumstances where it might have been a life-or-death situation for the loser was in poor taste. Melvin caught up to Morgan and his men the next day and likely had some choice words for them, though by this time the food had been lost in a capsizing accident.

The men were able to keep their good spirits and forward-looking mentality for a surprisingly long time. Through thick and thin along both the Kennebec and Dead Rivers, they persevered with aplomb and wit. It was only when the food began to run out that desperation began to set in. Some quit and some stole but all found the worst within themselves as hunger began to take its toll. "I am certain that if their bellies were full, they would be willing eno' to advance,"[10] wrote one captain. When food ran out, so did morale and order. For the first several days of November there was little to no food for the army, and had relief not come when it did a far higher death count would have been the result. But by this point, there was no alternative: they had to keep going. Attempting to return would have meant certain death.

Chapter 10: The Upper Chaudière

"Every boat we put into the river was stove in one part or another"[1] – John Henry

The word "Chaudière" means "caldron" in French, as in a boiling, seething mass of water. I was prepared for the worst: expedition journals tell a horror story for those still in boats and the Canadian border guard had also forebodingly warned me of the river. By all accounts it was going to be a doozy.

It was with significant surprise, then, that as I made my way down the river I saw no water spouts, whirlpools, or three-headed monsters. The upper sections of the Chaudière were surprisingly tame, populated mostly with those yellow construction booms and rocks. Fields of rocks. Forests of rocks. There were rocks on top of rocks, all emerging out of the water. There appeared to be more rocks than water, in most places. Where Arnold had descended the river on the tail of a hurricane, likely at near flood conditions, I was descending it in August at very low water. It was an entirely different river and, as I climbed out of my canoe for the umpteenth time within the first half-mile to drag around a rock and through a shallow spot, I began to have doubts about continuing.

Not, however, due to water levels. A little extra dragging and walking and a little less paddling never ruined a canoeing trip of mine. What bothered me was that every time I stepped out of the boat I was stepping into an oil slick – the very pollution that all these yellow booms were trying to clean up. The explosions in the town of Lac Megantic upstream had resulted in thousands of gallons of oil sloughing into the river and drifting downstream. I was literally navigating through a man-made rainbow. Did it make sense to continue through an oil-infested river? Would it be healthy? Would it be fun? I continued moving forward as I mulled it over, dodging the now-ubiquitous yellow booms and passing yet another clean-up crew, and equivocated.

· · ·

Arnold's army, on the other hand, was single-minded in its purpose: get to relief. But as the men rounded the corner of Lac Megantic and emerged at the source of the Chaudière, they came upon a scene of destruction. Morgan and his

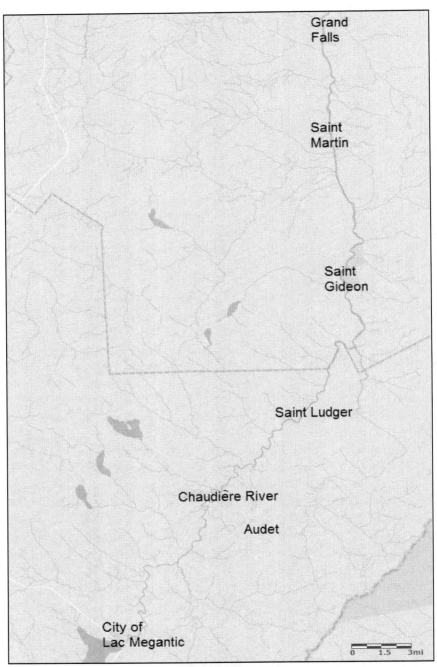

The Upper Chaudière

men, who had carried their boats across the height of land at such a cost, lay sprawled along the shore. They had been sucked into a particularly fierce rapid, "dashed on rocks," and had lost all their boats with one man drowned. "Their condition was truly deplorable," wrote Abner Stocking upon seeing the desperate group. "They had not when we came up with them a mouthful of provisions of any kind, and we were not able to relieve them, as hunger stared us in the face."[2] Senter concurred, writing that they lost "every thing except their lives, which they all saved by swimming," (a skill not taken for granted in the 18th century).[3] Morgan would eventually pull his company together and join the marchers trudging along the Chaudière's banks.

For there were very few paddlers left on the Chaudière. Morgan's wrecked bateaux meant that only Arnold's party in the vanguard was on the water. He had entered the Chaudière, "which is very Rapid, full of Rocks & dangerous, & the more so to us as we had no Guides," several days before anybody else. "We lashed our Baggage to the Boats, & the current carried us down the stream at the rate of eight or ten miles an hour," he bragged, making excellent time. But in a preview of Morgan's fate several days later, the river had its way with them as well. "We came to a very long rapid in which we had the misfortune to overset & stave 3 boats – lost all the Baggage, Arms, & Provisions of 4 men, & stove two of the Boats to pieces ag[ainst] the rocks." Ruing their misfortune, Arnold changed his mind after what followed. "We must think [the wreck] a very happy circumstance to the whole, & kind interposition of Providence for no sooner were the men dry & we embarked to proceed, but one of the men who was forward cried out a fall ahead which we had never been apprised of, & had we been carried over must inevitably have been dashed to pieces & all lost." They portaged around this larger rapid, and then "entered again on the river but with more precaution than before."[4] As a percentage, the Chaudière River was far more costly to boats and equipment than either the Dead or the Kennebec Rivers.

Henry describes another fortuitous circumstance paddling on the river. A crew transporting a sick soldier via boat, "although worthy men and well acquainted with such kind of navigation, knew nothing of this river. – They descended, unaware of the pitch before them, until they had got nearly into the ruck of the falls," he described. Out of potential calamity reared fortune's head. "Here, luckily, a rock presented itself, on which it was so contrived as to lodge the boat."[5] After this particular incident the crew forsook the river and returned to land. Arnold, however, managed to continue down the Chaudière, portaging frequently. His remaining boats were among the select few still seaworthy.*

---

* In yet another coincidence between Arnold's trip and Frank and Parker's, Frank described to me a similar incident. They were camped below the dam on the Chaudière which had a night release. They had neglected to pull their boats far enough from the water's edge, and one escaped downstream as

. . .

    I too was contemplating leaving the water, and the trip. Coming upon yet another clean-up crew, I stopped to try and get a better idea of the extent of the damage. The crew chief came down to the water's edge to meet me as I pulled in and, though we spoke in French, I'll relay the conversation in English.

    "Good afternoon," I said. He surely knew right away I was not local – not too many local paddlers on an oil-slicked river – but my accent must have confirmed it.

    "You are, uh, canoeing on this river?" he asked dubiously.

    I grinned. "Yes, it's my vacation! I'm from Vermont and I came up here to go paddling." Describing my re-creation of Arnold's trip was beyond my French so I left it at that.

    He shook his head. "Bad time to do it."

    I concurred and then begged some drinking water off him. I had neglected to fill up in the town of Lac Megantic, not realizing the situation on the river, and was now regretting it. We walked up the slope to their tent and rest station, leaving the crew spread out along the bank.

    "How far down does this go?" I asked, gesturing at the men and women working. They were currently power washing the river banks. A pump rested on a black inner tube and floated in the water. Attached to it was a hose which the operator held and directed at the bank. Leaves, dirt, grass and presumably oil were bombarded with the resultant stream of water and then washed into the river. The yellow booms then corralled it downstream of the work site – they must have had some sort of oil-absorbent material within.

    "For the next ten kilometers," he replied. "We've got 200 people working the river."

    "Ten kilometers," I thought to myself. "I can do this." I would stay with the trip, endure the oil, and see it through to the end. Like Arnold and his men, there would be no backing out for me (although by this point they of course did not have much of a choice).

    I thanked him profusely for the water and information and returned to my canoe. "Enjoy your vacation," he said sardonically, shaking his head as we parted ways. As I shoved off the whole crew stopped and watched. "Crazy American!" I could read across their faces.

    The water was opaque – the colors of the rainbow skittering across a sea

---

they slumbered. Luckily, it too, although unmanned, lodged on a rock just above Grand Falls. When Frank and Parker woke the next morning they raced downstream to find it, spotting it silhouetted through the falls' mist against the sky. It made a remarkable photograph and yet another similarity between their trips across the centuries.

of brown from all the sediment being washed into the river. Visibility was limited to a fraction of an inch downwards. As I thread my way between rocks the poor visibility made my job harder – it was tough to tell where the deep water was.

The yellow booms came every hundred yards or so, some more frequently, others less so. Some crossed only ¾ of the river, meaning that if I hugged one shore or the other I could simply duck the rope holding them in place and continue on. But many others covered the breadth of the river, necessitating a stop each time. I would head towards shore, climb into the oily water that was hopefully only shin deep (remember visibility was negligible), and then drag the canoe over the boom before clambering in on the other side. My pants, boots, and the inside of the canoe all became slippery, and I began to stink of oil. "Only ten kilometers," I kept chanting to myself, hoping the mantra would make the booms end all the quicker. Mostly I just focused on not falling into the water as I clambered back and forth. I must have been a sight, trying to balance in the canoe as I felt tentatively with my foot at the water's edge for a toehold to stand on. At one point, finding the water too deep, I precariously balanced on a boom and slowly hauled the canoe over it while tottering back and forth trying to steady myself. It worked but, deciding the risk was too great of oil submersion, I vowed to not use that technique again. It would just have to be slow going.

I soon drank all the water the crew had given me – they were using bottled water and had had a limited supply themselves – and began to look for a source. The Chaudière was of course off limits but any of the feeder streams entering it should be more or less clean, I reasoned. I picked one that, according to my map, appeared to be coming from the hills and not a farm, and stopped and filled my water bottles. Soon after I made camp for my first night on the Chaudière.

Shopping for food in Canada is always a little different. Jelly, for example, is not nearly as easy to come by nor as cheap as it is in the States. But I still supped on pasta and broke my fast on oatmeal. The brands were simply different. It didn't help that I had not stopped in Lac Megantic due to the frenetic construction and so was forced to resupply later in a miniscule town at a convenience store. Prices were high and options slim but I made do.

Dinner was spaghetti, the staple of many canoe trips. I used the water from the feeder stream for cooking since I had not camped near another source, and went to bed. It was actually one of my prettier campsites despite the poor water quality: I was camped in a cedar swamp, the pleasant aroma of which successfully combatted the smell of oil from the river.

Perhaps what I was most thankful for as I mulled over the events of the day, was that this was out of the ordinary. The rivers of New England and Canada abound with fish and are by and large healthy, vibrant, and pulsing with life. Soon, perhaps, the Chaudière too would be rejuvenated and returned to the ranks of healthy rivers. Many of the rivers of the world are not like that.

Recently I had watched a video of a man paddling through Los Angeles on the Los Angeles River. He took an inflatable boat through what has become a man-made river, complete with cement riverbed and banks. It more resembled a flowing canal than a river. Trash dotted the sides and graffiti artists had turned parts of the blank cement tableau into their version of art. The video was part of a campaign to work to rejuvenate the river. To me, it looked more like a funeral service. That river seemed beyond the hope of redemption.

The Chaudière brought to my mind shades of images from that video. But it was not as far gone. With efforts like the massive one I had just paddled through, it will return to its former glory. Even as I lay there in the cedar swamp that night, I could picture the river as it once was. Darkness covered up the oil slick and sedimentation, and with no lights or noise from civilization impeding my thoughts, I went to bed happy with only the burble of the river and smell of cedar in my nostrils. The challenges I had faced were certainly unexpected but I was committed to moving forward and completing the trip. I knew that this past day and the next would be among my most unpleasant of the journey. Ironically, they were also the worst for Arnold and his men as well.

. . .

"It is remarkable of this river, and which distinguished it from all others I had seen, that for 60 or 70 miles, it is a continued rapid, without any apparent gap or passage, even for a canoe," wrote John Henry, and indeed, the army was now primarily on foot.[6] Ordinarily not an issue – most armies traveled on foot of course – this particular army was on its last legs. It was early November in Canada, and snow coated the ground. They had been placed on half rations nearly three weeks prior, and divided the little remaining food back in Beautiful Meadow. With haggard appearance, growling bellies, and complete exhaustion hovering nearby, merely existing was not to be taken for granted, let alone making actual progress. Yet march they did.

It was not a pretty sight. "We were scattered up and down the river at the distance of perhaps twenty miles," noted Isaac Senter, writing that the breadth of the army was attributed to varying degrees of strength and health.[7] "Many of the company were so weak that they could hardly stand on their legs," agreed Abner Stocking. "When we attempted to march, they reeled about like drunken men."[8] Ironically having run out of alcohol weeks prior, the men would likely have counted themselves lucky had the swaying been due to excess libation.

The state of their clothing, particularly their footwear, did not help matters. "Our men proceed'd down the River, tho, in poor Circumstances, for Travelling, a Great Number of them being Barefoot, and the Weather Cold and Snowy" moaned Henry Dearborn.[9] James Melvin concurred, writing that "I had gone barefoot these two or three days, and wore my feet sore."[10] It snowed the entirety of the following day, undoubtedly increasing his pain. John Henry had a similar problem, and resorted to the only resource available to mend his shoes. "Bark, the only succedaneum for twine or leather in this miserable country, was immediately procured, and the shoe bound tightly to the foot."[11] Yet the footwear problem paled in comparison to their universal complaint. They were out of food.

After the distribution in Beautiful Meadow, each man had his apportioned provisions for the remainder of the journey. Each could do with it what he liked – whether attempting to ration it as far as it would go, or eating it immediately all at once. Those that rationed fared better. "Our greatest luxuries now consisted in a little water, stiffened with flour, in imitation of shoemakers' paste, which was christened with the name of Lillipu," narrated Dr. Senter.[12] Henry called the same mixture "bleary,"[13] but whatever name it went by, it was all that was left of the rations to eat. Henry also described how they ate the bits of distributed pork, putting them in a camp kettle "with each man's bit of pork, distinctly marked by running a small skewer of wood through it, with his particular and private designation."[14] This allowed for some broth to go with the meat. "One of our Company had a small bit of chocolate," wrote Mathias Ogden thankfully, "which we boiled and divided out equally by spoonfuls."[15] Every spoonful counted, and likely every man was watched by many hungry eyes as he downed his allotted portion.

It was not a lot. "Each man had not more Provision for the 4 Days than he Could Comfortable eat at one meal,"[16] lamented John Pierce, the surveyor. As men will do in such a situation, bargaining began fiercely. "Our hunger was so great that many offered dollars for a single mouthful of bread,"[17] remembered Stocking. Even in those days when a dollar had much more value than it does now, one suspects that not too many deals were actually struck, such were their circumstances.

Indeed, there were those men who gobbled it all down at once, in the hope that fate would intervene in their favor later on. "I was told that some of the soldiers, who ate their whole allowance the morning after our provisions were divided in the wilderness, were obliged, in order to sustain life, to eat their dogs, cartridge-boxes, old shoes, and clothes,"[18] wrote Simeon Fobes. He was not wrong, and to the modern day reader some seemed to make almost a macabre game of trying to digest inedibles. "No one can imagine who hath not experienced it, the sweetness of a roasted shot-pouch to the famished appetite,"[19] noted George Morison. Senter dined on candles one meal and another enjoyed a barber's powder bag.

Still others appear to be writing recipes for publication. "Taking up some raw-hides, that lay for several Days in the bottom of their boats…and chopping them to pieces, singeing first the hair, afterwards boiling them and living on the juice or liquid that they soak'd from it for a considerable time."[20] Or, as someone else might write about a steak: marinate, dice, sauté, and simmer before eating. "Our bill of fare for last night and this morning," wrote Senter, sounding as if he were reviewing a fine dining establishment, "consisted of the jawbone of a swine destitute of any covering. This we boiled in a quantity of water, that with a little thickening constituted our sumptuous eating."[21] Later he wrote that, "Nor did the shaving soap, pomatum, and even the lip salve, leather of their shoes, cartridge boxes, &c., share any better fate."[22] Only the lead musket balls seemed to manage to escape attempted digestion.

One particularly heart-wrenching event was the consumption of the division's pets. Dearborn had brought his dog along for the journey, who appeared to be universally loved by all the men. Yet the day came when he too joined the food pot. Dearborn himself writes about it matter-of-factly. "This day Cap[tain] Goodrich's Company Kill'd my Dog, and another dog, and Eat them."[23] After consuming every part of him, they pounded up his bones and made a broth of them as well. Two other dogs shared a similar end.

While the men attempted to put a lighter note on their difficulties (Senter wrote one of the funnier asides when he wryly noted that "Cooking being very much out of fashion [due to lack of food to actually cook], we had little else to do than march"[24]), they were in a deadly serious situation. Some modern-day readers have questioned the above descriptions, noting that while some seem to be on death's door for days on end, other journalists make little note of starvation. It is important to remember that the army was spread out across dozens of miles. Even after the universal rendez-vous and rationing at Beautiful Meadow, the army was soon spread out again. Some companies were better at rationing than others, and some reached relief quicker than others. What is clear is that these were confused, desperate days, with each man physically and emotionally exhausted. Some did not make it. "This day I passed a number of soldiers who had no provisions, and some that were sick, and not in my power to help or relieve them, except to encourage them,"[25] wrote Return Meigs, a division commander. Others seemed to shine in the moment. Aaron Burr, like Arnold later famous for his own treasonous activities, was one of these. He was noted by several for his tenacity and endurance in spite of his small size. While others were too enfeebled to go on, he still possessed a surprising energy and verve.

It was each man for himself. The following spring Simeon Fobes returned to the banks of the Chaudière (he escaped from captivity and eventually made his way back to Maine via the Dead and Kennebec across the same way the army had entered Quebec). "We came upon human bones and hair scattered about on the ground promiscuously. It was doubtless the spot where some of our fellow soldiers perished the Fall before on their way to Quebec."[26] Estimates vary but likely somewhere in the neighborhood of forty men died in the final days before reaching the southernmost French settlements.

. . .

The first morning on the Chaudière I woke, made breakfast among the cedars, and then took my daily bowel movement. Afterwards, I turned to bury it and found to my surprise and distress that it contained some red in it. Nothing had changed but my water sources so, worried that that was indeed the cause of the blood, I swore off both water directly taken from the Chaudière as well as from its tributaries. Canadian water simply could not be trusted. I vowed to keep an eye on the situation – I didn't feel sick or ill but I certainly knew that blood in my stool was not a good thing – and looked over my maps for the next town where I could get fresh water.

Unfortunately the next town directly on the water was Saint Ludger, which would not come for quite some time. I needed water quicker than that. Much sooner, however, I would cross under a bridge with a road that led to a town perhaps 7 kilometers away. Perhaps I could hitchhike.

I climbed into the canoe and made for the bridge. All day would be one continuous merry-go-round of clambering in and out of the boat. Where Henry had described 60 miles of continuous rapids, I faced what felt like 60 miles of continuous rock gardens and oil boom lattice-works. In and out, in and out I climbed, sometimes paddling no more than a couple feet before beaching again on another rock or facing another blockading yellow boom. As tiresome as it was, it kept me warm in the drizzle which showed no signs of stopping.

I reached the bridge mid-morning. Hiding my canoe and gear in some nearby brush, I climbed up the abutment to a quiet stretch of road. Looking left and right, the road petered out into the distance in both directions. Dead quiet ruled and nothing disturbed the dust. Feeling like a cowboy who walks into a town only to find it deserted, I decided to wait for a bit. Perhaps a car would come. Sure enough, in a couple minutes, a car crested the horizon. Dubious that anyone would pick me up in damp, odorous paddling clothes, I nevertheless stuck my thumb out when the car zoomed by. No luck. Silence returned and I grinned half-heartedly to myself – the gray sky and breeze kicking up the dust only reinforced the first impression of a deserted stretch of road. It could be a while.

But it took only two more cars, each spaced a couple of minutes apart, before a younger man stopped. I explained my needs as best I could, emphasizing "l'épicerie" several times, as well as the town of "Audet". It seemed to work because in ten minutes he dropped me off at the convenience store in town, telling me that this was the best there was.

It was good enough for me. I bought bread, pasta, tomato sauce, and a few other necessities from the nearly empty shelves – a common affliction of small town general stores found too often in the States as well as Canada – before walking next store to the "Cantine" or snack bar. There I enjoyed a hot chicken, bacon and egg sandwich. Why we don't serve fried eggs on top of sandwiches more often south of the border I will never know because it is a tradition I love. I savored every bit, enjoying it as much because it was made by someone besides myself crouched over a campfire as because it was delicious. The woman working the stove was kind enough to fill up my water bottle as well.

We had taken several turns to get to Audet from the bridge so I was nervous that a hitch back wouldn't take me the whole way in one ride. Yet once again I was fortunate enough to get a quick ride all the way to the river. Between my two rides and the owners of the convenience store and the snack bar I had met some very friendly individuals. It was nice to have some human interactions with people who didn't just stare at me as I paddled past, as the clean-up crews had.

No one had bothered my hidden boat or gear so I reloaded and, with coffers, water jugs and belly full and spirits renewed, I set off downstream.

. . .

Arnold overcame numerous portages, linings, and other obstacles, at one time with the help of "two Penobscot Indians who appeared friendly & assisted us"[27] around Grand Falls. Several miles below the falls, he at last reached the southernmost settlements along the Chaudière near the junction with the Rivière du Loups, at what he called Sartigan (the name actually refers to the region, not a town, but for Arnold's sake we'll name it as he did). Arnold had made it out of the wilderness, but his men were still spaced out behind him, struggling to catch up.

He immediately dispatched relief back upstream, hiring locals guided by some of the soldiers with him to hurry cattle, flour, oatmeal, and other provisions to his starving men. It would take two more days before relief reached the foremost soldiers.

On November 2nd, Dr. Isaac Senter saw a strange sight. "A vision of horned cattle, four footed beasts, &c. rode and drove by animals resembling Plato's two footed featherless ones." No doubt shaking his head to clear his vision, it persisted. "Upon a nigher approach our vision proved real! Exclamations of joy. – Echoes of gladness resounded from front to rear!" Relief had been found at last! "Each man was restricted to one pound of beef," Senter wrote. Food was needed for men further back, and besides, gorging would only result in sickness. So they sat down, "blessed our stars, and thought it a luxury." The relief party continued "up the river in order to the rear's partaking of the same benediction." Arnold's army had beaten the wilderness.[28]

Others, unsurprisingly, had similar experiences of wonder and joy at sighting the cattle lowing their way towards them. "It Caus[ed] the Tears to Start from my Eyes,"[29] wrote Dearborn, sighting relief just before reaching Grand Falls. "This was the most joyful sight our eyes ever beheld," agreed Stocking. Most stopped immediately to partake of the new food, many not even cooking the food and instead eating the beef and grains raw. "I got a little piece of the flesh, which

I eat raw with a little oat meal wet with cold water," wrote Stocking of his relief meal, "and thought I feasted sumptuously."[30]

Their experimentation with edibles seemed to continue, however. After eating their allotted one pound of beef, and upon watching the relief move upstream towards other men, some were still hungry. Henry watched one man, "gorging the last bit of a colon, half rinsed – half broiled. It may be said he ate with pleasure."[31] Simeon Fobes, feeling the same hunger, wrote that "I had the good fortune to get hold of a piece of an intestine five or six inches long; this I washed, threw it on the coals for a short time, and then ate it with relish." With slight irony he wrote afterwards, "Such is the appetite of hunger."[32] It would be several days before their strength began to return and their stomachs began to feel full again.

But they could not rest. The weather continued to threaten, and every day lost on the march was another day that the British might find out their plans and fortify Quebec more strongly. So after a quick meal they continued on. Grand Falls was just above Sartigan, "which are of astonishing height and exhibit an awful appearance."[33] As the army was on foot, it provided no obstacle, however.

Sighting the first humble abodes of the rural French created a whole new cause for celebration. "About two o'clock we espied a house – then we gave three huzzas, for we have not seen a house before for thirty days," celebrated Caleb Haskell.[34] Stocking seems to have summed up the general sentiment when he compared it to the end of a jail sentence. "It was like being brought from a dungeon to behold the clear light of the sun."[35]

However it felt, they couldn't bask in it for long. Arnold, after seeing to the relief party, was already looking forward towards Quebec and the anticipated assault. Spurring the army onwards, the men must have quickly thanked their Quebec rescuers, resignedly risen to their feet, and continued the march. It snowed hard again on November 3rd, which must have only quickened their step. There would be no rest for the weary.

. . .

I, however, was taking all the rest I wanted. I was ahead of schedule and, since I was not meeting Sarah, my ride home from Quebec, for a week more, I could enjoy the river. The river, in turn, was finally allowing me to enjoy it.

The yellow booms must have been working, at least a little bit. The oily smell began to dissipate and then disappear from the water. No longer was the surface a myriad of colors. As additional tributaries entered the main channel, the water began to deepen and slow so that I did not need to dodge emergent rocks every couple of feet. And simultaneously the booms became more and more infrequent until they only barred passage every couple of miles. I even became a little nostalgic for their ubiquitous presence. But only a little.

In place of cedar swamp shores and an uninhabited, untouched littoral zone, I began to enter an actively farmed region. The smell of manure replaced the oil, and farmhouses dotted the shores with hay fields abutting the river banks. I spotted an occasional tree farm as well, and after reaching Saint Ludger, I passed through towns every ten or so miles.

I stopped in Saint Gideon's one morning, hoping for a hot meal. But I was too early by several hours – things open late in small town Canada – so I simply dumped my trash in a handy waste barrel and continued on. Saint Martin I hit at mid-day so I bought a box of cookies – nearly eating the whole thing – and some ice cream. Life on the trail means, for myself anyways, experiencing cravings for cold food and drink. An iced soda, cold beer or ice cream all seem to really hit the spot when most meals have only tepid or hot items. The ice cream disappeared quickly.

On the water I did a lot of half-hearted paddling while watching the shore go slowly by. I had mapped out where I needed to camp each night to stay on schedule and, with the current moving as it was, I hardly needed to paddle to reach each day's destination. I took long lunches on shore, and enjoyed the scenery. And on the water, I had fun.

One of my favorite activities was to try to sneak up on a flock of geese. The Canadian goose is a surprisingly observant animal, and in spite of my nonchalant approach, I never got too close. I'd even talk aloud, trying to reassure them I meant no harm. "Don't mind me, I'm just drifting downstream. Not bothering anybody. Ho hum. Lah-di-dah. What a pleasant day for a paddle. I have no bad intentions with you geese, don't mind me." I got so I could recognize the signal that one of them would finally give – a ruffling of their wings and a certain jerk of the neck – before the whole gaggle would take flight (which, for those so interested, means they lose "gaggle" status and become a "skein" or "wedge"). I whipped out my camera a couple of times to take pictures of their wings batting the water as they erupted into the sky.

I also started a conversation with a blue heron who was leading me downstream. He was posted sentry-like on shore and, as I neared him, would awkwardly unfurl his wings and lift off. I thanked him for guiding my way and keeping an eye on me. Soon, however, I got too off-hand with him, teasing him with names like "birdbrain" and "featherbutt". He must have taken offense because soon after the name-calling began, I lost sight of him.

Grand Falls appeared the morning of my 12th day. Arnold's men, upon reaching this point, had all reached relief but not yet any settlements. As noted before, they admired its fierceness. Frank and Parker in the 1970s also remembered its beauty so I was looking forward to the sight. It did not disappoint. The river dropped over some upper ledges before shooting through a bottleneck and falling a couple dozen feet. I looked for the rock that lodged Frank and Parker's boat (remember they had let a boat drift downstream one night only to find it wedged just above the falls) as well as perhaps Arnold's but couldn't definitively decide upon one.

I portaged briefly on river right around a couple of the upper ledges before putting in and hugging the shore until just above the falls. Then a second portage, this time on river left, on exposed ledge around the falls proper before running the fallout below. Thrilled as I was to able to run many of the rips on either side of the falls, albeit by hugging the shore and moving slowly, I was even more pleased to have an observer. The falls runs through a deep gorge with steep cliffy walls on either side. Perched at the top of one was a house jutting out towards the river with a clear view of the cataract. A man stood on the porch, enjoying what must have been his usual routine of coffee with a view. With the roar of the cascading water, verbal communication would have been impossible even had the distance been closer. But as I looked up at him he raised his cup in acknowledgement. I fancied he admired my navigation, but I also think he was simply surprised to see someone on the river – the Chaudière is not a popular paddling river, especially after a recent oil spill. Pleased with my success and enjoying the river, I continued downstream.

The only gray cloud in my sky was my gastro-intestinal system. I had had blood in my BM for three mornings in a row now and was getting nervous. It had never happened to me before, and given my water drinking habits and lack of filtration, I was nervous I had picked something up. My girlfriend Elizabeth is a medical student but she would probably throw a fit if I gave her the news so instead I called a good friend, another med student, who would take a much more sensible tone.

"Oh yeah. You're fine," he said. "Don't worry about it – people have that all the time. Happens to me too sometimes. You feel okay?"

"I feel fine," I replied, but was still worried. "But it's never happened to *me* before. You don't think some bad water, or oil, or something could have…"

"You feel okay - then you are okay," he cut me off. "If it's not gone in a couple of weeks then maybe see somebody about it. But don't sweat it. Enjoy the trip." And indeed, a couple of days later the problem disappeared. It's nice to have so sensible a friend.

I did make a decision around this time, however. Several days of taking it slow, drifting occasionally, and enjoying a lunchtime nap had been nice, but I was getting antsy. I called Sarah and asked if she could come early.

"How about Friday?" she asked. That was two days earlier than planned, which would work perfectly. Feeling gung-ho, I also decided to spend an extra day in Quebec, exploring the city. So from a very sedate pace I switched to a fast one. It was time to make some miles! Arnold's men, reinvigorated with food and energy, pushed hard for Quebec City from Grand Falls, attempting to surprise the British. I would do the same.

Interlude: The Quebecois

""We have been very kindly received by the inhabitants who appear very friendly and willing to supply us with provisions."[1] – Benedict Arnold

B enedict Arnold and his men had marched and paddled over two hundred miles to reach the first Quebec settlements. Emerging from the wilderness starving, fatigued, and in some cases, very near death, they were in no shape to fight a battle, let alone win one. So the ultimate question for many was, how would they be received by the French settlers living in the first villages? Would they be friendly and helpful, or hostile? More importantly, were their sufferings at an end, or would they have to fight simply to get food to survive? And finally, would the French aid them in their attempt to conquer Quebec, or were the inhabitants loyal to the king?

Early reports all pointed towards the former. "The French Inhabitants appear very friendly & were rejoiced to hear of our approach," a scout returning from the settlements reported to Arnold.[2] And indeed, when Arnold first reached the settlements and told the villagers there of his army's predicament, all sources seem to say that the French dropped whatever they were doing, loaded up cattle and supplies, and started back upriver immediately in support. Arnold's purse no doubt greased the wheels of relief but there seem to have been no hesitations on the part of the French to aid the invading soldiers.

As the French relief parties met the soldiers heading north, and as soldiers entered the first villages, surprise and curiosity seems to have been present on both sides. For the villagers' part, they "looked upon us in amazement; and seemed to doubt whether or not we were human beings," wrote George Morison. "To see a number of famished creatures, more like ghosts than men, issuing from a dismal Wilderness, with arms in their hands, was the most astonishing sight they ever beheld."[3] Rumors of the invading army must have reached them prior to the soldiers' arrival, but it certainly was still a strange sight to behold for the rural farmers.

The Americans were no less surprised by the French. "Where I expected there could be little other than barbarity, we found civilized men in a comfortable state,"[4] remembered John Henry. Abner Stocking was equally surprised at their civility. "The kindness and hospitality of the inhabitants, was to us very pleasing. After having been lately our enemies, at war with us, we did not expect to experience from them to[o] much friendship."[5] Henry Dearborn found them uneducated but friendly. "The people are ignorant but are very kind to us."[6] Overall, it was a very friendly introduction between cultures.

Dearborn's comment on ignorance was likely the result of those cultural differences. The French inclination towards devout Catholicism in particular amazed the Americans. "Not one in 400 that could read one word but [all] were very Precise in Saying their Prayers Counting their Beads and Crossing themselves," wrote one soldier, expressing his surprise that even the minister extended his generosity towards the American and Protestant soldiers.[7] John Henry was equally amazed at the open-mindedness of the Catholic inhabitants. A fellow soldier passed away soon after reaching the settlements. "His corpse received a due respect from the inhabitants of the vicinage," Henry wrote. "This real Catholicism towards the remains of one we loved, made a deep and wide breach upon my early prejudices, which since that period has caused no regret, but has induced a more extended and paternal view of mankind, unbounded by sect or opinion."[8] While his sentiments are no doubt overstated here, one gets the gist of the interactions.

Some historians have accused the Quebecois of acting solely in their own self-interest. What better market for their produce and meat than starving soldiers? Some narratives do indeed seem to point towards this conclusion. The first day among the French, Simeon Thayer wrote, "We got a little repast and paid very dear for it." The following entry he again noted that, "The people were civil, but mighty extravagant with what they have to sell."[9] But were they taking advantage of the Americans?

It must be remembered that it was November, directly before the onset of the brutal Canadian winter. The snow was already flying. The Canadians were selling the Americans what might be badly needed provisions come the end of March. These were the stores they had spent all summer setting by for the winter months. The extravagant prices were necessary to ensure that if they did run out of food, they themselves could purchase more and wouldn't starve during the winter.

Regardless, it would be tough to fault the Canadians for raising their prices slightly. It was indeed a seller's market, after all. Thayer himself found a similar situation back on the Kennebec amongst fellow Americans when he wrote "The people are courteous and breathe nothing but liberty. Their produce, (they sell at an exorbitant price)."[10] His comment could have been transplanted a month later in his journal and no one would have noticed. Perhaps Thayer was simply a bit of a skinflint. By and large, the Canadians treated the Americans with more than generosity, feeding, clothing, and housing the sick, sometimes even refusing payment for doing so. "Had we been in New-England among people of our own nation," summed up Stocking, "we should not, I think, have been treated with more kindness."[11]

While the common soldier was thankful for simply being out of the wilderness, ("I last night lodged in a house,"[12] wrote Stocking, his emphasis), Arnold had other matters on his mind. Part of his orders was to attempt to recruit some of the Canadians to the Continental army. "You are to endeavor…to conciliate the Affections of those People & such Indians as you may meet with by every Means in your Power – convincing them that we Come at the Request of many of their Principal People, not as Robbers or to make War upon them but as Friends & Supporters of their Liberties as well as ours,"[13] Washington wrote before the expedition left. He carried manifestoes and written proclamations, printed in Boston prior to departure, through the wilderness in the hopes that these would help sway the locals, and also no doubt made speeches and met with many of the local leaders.

It was mostly for naught. The Canadians were firmly entrenched in their highly structured system of class distinction. While not particularly pleased that the British were ruling their country – Canada had been ceded to the English from the French after the French & Indian War – the British had since proceeded with a fairly enlightened administration of the country, leaving the Catholic inhabitants to much their own devices. With no heritage of disobedience or revolution, the inertia was simply too overwhelming for Arnold and the Americans to overcome.

The British did their part to convince the Canadians to not actively aid the Americans or take up arms. Guy Carleton, Governor of Quebec, knowing that there was no love lost between the French peasants and British rulers, perhaps sensibly doubted the allegiance of the Canadians. So he threatened anyone found taking up arms against the crown with imprisonment and destruction of house and home. Given the ragtag appearance of the American army upon emergence from the wilds, it's little wonder that few Canadians decided to risk all for the patriot cause. The army could not have instilled great confidence among the locals regarding their chances of success.

So the Canadians, while friendly and hospitable to the utmost degree, would do little to add to the army's numbers. As Arnold and his men made their way down the Chaudière, they would again and again be amazed at the generosity and sympathy of the inhabitants. And meanwhile, some Canadians did actually join, especially as the army finally reached Quebec and began the siege of the city. Shortsightedly, Carleton ordered anyone not willing to take up arms against the Americans out of the city, an offer that a number of Quebecois took him up on. Many of these exiles decided to join the invaders. But the peasantry along the river would largely remain at their stoops. Arnold could reasonably have expected no more – with their generosity of food and consideration they had almost singlehandedly saved his army. The Americans *lived to fight another day and as they gained strength on Canadian beef and grain, they continued northwards towards Quebec City and their ultimate goal.*

Chapter 11: The Lower Chaudière, Etchemin, and Saint Lawrence Rivers

"In open sight of the enemy, nought but the river divided us."[1] – Dr. Isaac Senter

With a new schedule and plan, I could now push hard towards my goal of Quebec City. No more chasing geese or imitating ducks (as fun as it was) for me. As the Chaudière transitioned from a large stream to a broad river, in addition to increased farm activity on its banks it began to flatten out. Above Grand Falls I had been paddling nearly continuous Class I and II rapids. Below Grand Falls I hit the occasional rapid, but increasingly it was simply swifts, or just flat water.

One solitary ledge did send me for a swim – the first and only of the trip. It was a short drop, perhaps three feet, and I chose a good line. But on a sharp turn amidst bedrock protruding from the water I bounced off a rock, dipped a gunwale and went over. It was a hot day and with no damage done I was soon upright, bailed, and before lunch, dry as well. Most importantly, no one saw the spill, so it practically did not even count.

Overturning a canoe can result in mixed feelings. On this hot, sunny day with no consequences, it was of little matter and even provided a rush of adrenaline. I certainly chuckled and jokingly reprimanded myself afterwards. But it can be a huge hit to morale as well – on a cold rainy day where perhaps some food or clothing gets soaked it can make or break a day on the trip. The simple answer is to not let it hurt the spirits, acknowledge it as yet another part of canoe-tripping, enjoy the bath, and keep on moving. No sense in wallowing in self-pity or embarrassment (which for me is sometimes more easily said than done). On this day, it was barely a blip on my radar. Soon after I portaged the dam in Saint Georges, stopping for fresh water at a nearby gas station, and continued on.

. . .

While no longer paddling on the river, the expedition was pushing as hard as I was, if not harder. "This morning orders were given for every captain to

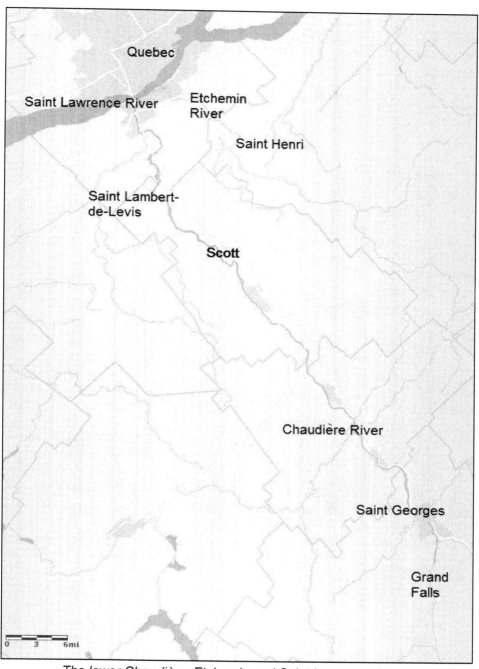

The lower Chaudière, Etchemin and Saint Lawrence Rivers

get his company on as fast as possible and not to leave a man behind unless unfit for duty," wrote Senter.[2] All haste was needed to catch Quebec City as unprepared as possible, while at the same time every man available was needed due to the low numbers and poor condition of the soldiery.

The Canadians remained helpful. Upon arriving in one village, Return Meigs wrote, "We were supplied with fresh beef, fowls, butter, pheasants, and vegetables."[3] This generosity of heart and goods provided much-needed sustenance for the marching army. The fresh beef even provided additional aid in the form of footwear. "As fast as the beefs were killed," noted the doctor, "the hides were made into savage shoes."[4] Cloth and leather were still at a premium for an army that was dressed mostly in rags.

Per the orders described above by Senter, some men did remain behind who were too ill to march. "So fatigued, that they were very unfit for action," documented Dearborn, "a Considerable number of our men are left on the road Sick or worn out with fatigue & hunger."[5] Some camped where they stopped, but many found hospitable Canadians with whom to lodge while they recuperated. A couple days of food and rest seemed to quickly revive most men and once the army stopped on the Saint Lawrence, most were able to catch up in a timely manner.

Had they been able to paddle, this section of river in particular would have been conducive to their needs: even men in their condition would have been able to safely navigate it. When Montresor traveled the river years earlier he noted, "The river in general is deep, with a moderate current; it has a few rifts, but they are not difficult." The lower sections, as I was finding, were in particular easily navigable. "Except in very dry seasons," Montresor recorded, "it is practicable for light batteaux."[6] A few did take advantage of the current, hiring local boats and paddlers to carry them downstream. Alas, it was not to be for most of the army. With no boats of their own, they remained on foot.

The road they were following left the Chaudière near present day Scott. The marching army would of course follow the road which cut due north diagonally between the two rivers before bumping into the Etchemin River and following it to its mouth on the banks of the St. Lawrence. The final leg of their journey, across open land on a road due to the loss of their bateaux, would create the hardest day of the trip for me 240 years later.

.   .   .

The morning of my thirteenth day on the water, I woke to cloudy skies and drizzle. It would soon become a driving, cold rain that would sustain itself for the remainder of the day on the strength of a stiff breeze, making what was already a challenging portage even tougher.

Duluth, Parker and Frank had all agreed that the last dozen or so miles

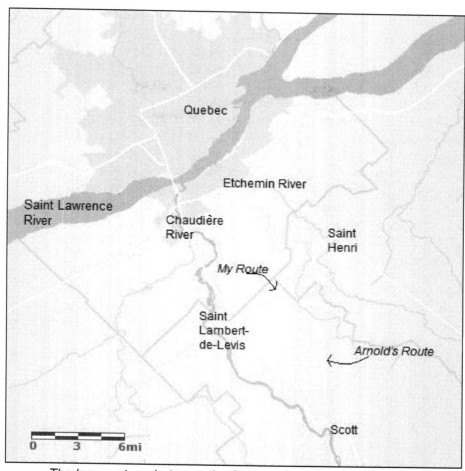

The long portage between the Chaudière and Etchemin Rivers

of the Chaudière, before it reached the St. Lawrence, were incredibly ledgy and difficult to navigate. Montresor in the 18th century concurred, writing that "It was intended at first to embark on the river Chaudière, which falls into the St. Lawrence on the south side about four miles above Quebec; but as the rapids and falls prevent it from being navigable for some leagues from its mouth, we were obliged to cross the country to St. Egan [present day Scott]." Benedict Arnold also did not travel the Chaudière north of Scott. He did not have boats anyways, but in an effort to deceive the British who by now had heard that he was traveling down the Chaudière, he followed Montresor's route over land to the Etchemin before continuing towards Quebec. Neither Arnold nor Montresor had paddled the Etchemin either – they were all on foot at this time. Having no interest in portaging my own canoe in the 21st century the rest of the way to Quebec, I would follow Arnold and switch rivers, but then put in and paddle down the Etchemin. Similar to my shadowing of his marching army along the Chaudière, I would paddle alongside the expedition as it marched the last few miles to the Saint Lawrence along the Etchemin.

The road that Arnold took between rivers, while the shortest distance in overall mileage, was actually a diagonal between the Chaudière and Etchemin, necessitating nearly fourteen miles of walking between leaving the Chaudière and sighting the Etchemin. For a paddler like myself with a canoe on his shoulders, this was not the most direct or shortest route between water bodies. So for the second time, I elected to make a significant re-route from Arnold's path.

Instead of leaving the river at Scott, I would continue northwards, still on the Chaudière, past the small town and take out another dozen miles downstream at Saint-Lambert-de-Levis. From there I could portage a shorter distance of eight miles to Saint Henri and the Etchemin River – at the same place that Arnold arrived at the Etchemin – and rejoin Arnold's route. It would save me 6 miles of portaging and omit none of the river miles (in fact adding some extra paddling on the Chaudière). It seemed like an eminently reasonable alternative to me. So that is exactly what I did.

The paddling up to Scott was as flat as could be, and I made excellent time. Soon after Scott, however, the river became much more problematic to successfully descend. Montresor and Arnold were indeed correct when they wrote that navigation became more difficult. Large swaths of ledge and bedrock created some odd river features, stretching across the channel from bank to bank. Great stretches of river were very shallow, and these challenging sections were occasionally broken up with larger drops between five and ten feet high. Even in good weather it would have been a trial.

With the wind and rain in my eyes, I put the best face on it I could. I enjoyed what I was able to, and endured the rest, battling swirling currents and jagged rocks to make progress downstream. It was not ideal paddling. Several times I forced to get out of the boat into the chilling waters to line the canoe over larger drops or across inch-deep water where the river was sheeting across bedrock. By the time I finally reached Saint-Lambert-de-Levis I was sodden, shivering, and worn. And it was only 11:00 AM.

I have endured a number of days like this one throughout my times on the water. They all consist of the same elements. There is always a headwind. Your rain coat is never waterproof enough. Your fingers always go numb. The hood of your raincoat prevents you from enjoying peripheral vision, which is very disconcerting. And you always wish you were somewhere else.

But make it I did. I huddled under the bridge that crossed the river, the road which would lead me the Etchemin. It would have been nice to have had someone to huddle with, but solitary canoe journeys make for lonely huddles. Guiding a group of teenagers some years prior, I remembered a similar day with the winds whipping in our faces and waves crashing over the bows. When we finally found a spot to camp for the night, we built a roaring fire, encircled it with our shivering bodies, and belted out Motown hits from the 70's to keep our spirits up. Periodically we'd turn 180 degrees to warm our backsides as well. I remember watching the boys smile through their clenched teeth as their voices rose in off-key song, their exuberance telling the world that though the weather was inclement, their morale was high.

Under a bridge was no place for a bonfire, even if I did have a group with me, so I was forced to come up with other ways of getting warm. Portaging certainly fit the bill. A long drink of water and a quick snack were only excuses to put off beginning the walk. So, with a "You've got this, Sam," to myself and a quick shake of my arms to warm them, I shouldered my pack and threw up my canoe.

The portage itself wasn't hard. Eight miles of nearly flat pavement, following Rte. 218 through rural developments and large farms, was fairly straightforward in and of itself. But all that farmland meant that trees were relatively scarce. The weather took advantage of this, blowing a strong wind across my path and buffeting the canoe ceaselessly. My right arm soon grew tired from trying to keep the canoe straight, and my left I was forced to keep perpetually locked. The only good thing was that the continual fight with the elements to maintain headway warmed me immediately.

I crossed over an interstate almost immediately, the winds picking up enough through the exposed position that I was half-afraid I would be lifted up and deposited in the middle of the freeway. Fortunately gravity maintained its precarious hold on me. Had any drivers taken their eyes from the road and looked up at me on the overpass, I suspect I might have caused an accident or two. As it was, the automobiles zipping by on the highway underneath seemed to mock my slow, agonized pace.

Route 218 is a fairly well-traveled road so I received unending stares from the drivers of passing automobiles, especially as I neared the middle of the portage. Walking along nearly four miles away from the large river, I must have been a surprising sight for the passing motorists. But only a truck with two younger fellows in it stopped to actually check on me.

"You okay?" one asked in English. Our proximity to the city meant that bi-linguicism was more frequent.

"Doing just fine," I thanked them, giving them the thumbs up.

"Where are you going?" the other asked disbelievingly.

"The Etchemin River, and Saint Henri," I responded. We were still perhaps six miles away. "I didn't like the Chaudière so I thought I'd switch things up a bit." I don't think they believed my joking answer, but they nodded and waved and drove off. An hour later I spotted them again. They'd come back to check on me, and finding me still among the living they simply slowed, waved, and honked in friendly support. Nice kids.

About two-thirds of the way through I reached a small river crossing under the road. More than wide and deep enough to paddle in, any sensible person would have stopped right there and put in. It led, after all, to the Etchemin. But it didn't meet the main river until several miles downstream from Saint Henri. I wanted to make sure I saw Saint Henri - Arnold did after all - so, defying all common sense, I kept walking.

I took two short five minute breaks along the way, disobeying my own rule (already broken, if you recall, on the first of the Great Carrying Place portages) of not stopping on portages. Eight miles was simply too long to walk without a rest somewhere along the way. Even still, the last mile was a challenge. I felt like an automaton, with my legs disjointed from my body and moving with a mind of their own. I could feel blisters beginning in my waterlogged boots and my hips and groin began to ache, but I kept walking.

A blinking yellow light signaled the T-junction of Route 218 and Routes 173/275. Off in the distance, it heralded the end of the trek and my tired body found one last reserve of strength to walk the last little bit. Just across the road from the junction lay the river and I dropped the canoe exhaustedly on the bank before collapsing back into it, with rain pelting my face and dripping down my spine. It had taken me a little less than three hours, and I was proud of the accomplishment – it was the longest portage I had ever done.

I felt like I could have lain there in the canoe on the grass forever. My body felt that beat. My feet were on fire and my hip flexors were sending Morse code signals upwards that they were not going to be operating for a while. But a lawn near the road in the pouring rain was no place to spend a lot of time. I could be brought in for loitering, for all I knew. So after letting the rain plaster my face for several minutes, I slowly sat upwards. Looking around for some sort of welcoming party or congratulatory committee on setting a new personal portaging record, I was of course disappointed. So, fighting aching joints and stiff legs, I loaded the gear into the boat and shoved off into a swiftly flowing stream. At least the rain meant that I shouldn't have any problems with the river being too shallow.

A short paddle further on the Etchemin brought me to Saint Henri. I stashed my canoe under yet another bridge and walked - perhaps hobbled is a better word - into town for a late lunch. My pace was certainly sedate and my gait far from elegant, we'll put it that way. A small café answered the call and I put away three sandwiches for lunch. They weren't even very good. The owner/chef simply looked on in horror at the speed with which I demolished his food.

Back on the river, I was confronted with a very different flow than the one I had left on the Chaudière. The Etchemin was much smaller and quicker river than the large, cumbersome Chaudière. Sliding around tight corners and dodging suddenly-appearing rocks, I felt back at home on the kind of river I love. My legs were safely at rest in the canoe and my arms were thrilled to be actively moving instead of braced against the gunwales. I think I actually let out a howl of joy as the river carried me swiftly downstream – it felt that good to be out there soaking up rain and attacking the river. The Chaudière I left was simply too bulky and cumbersome a body of water to bring the kind of surprises and excitement that I like in river.

I paddled for perhaps an hour before deciding to pack it in for the day. This close to Quebec, the population was only becoming denser and if I didn't take advantage of camping opportunities now, I might not find one. My final night on the river was on a low, swampy point, but I was too tired to care. I set up my tent and rolled immediately into it, wrapping my sleeping bag around me as the rain poured down outside, and simply laying there. It was heaven to be warm and dry. I dozed for a couple of hours before rising to cook a quick dinner – the rain finally slowed enough to mean that building a fire was an easy matter – and then promptly returning to the nest of my tent. I slept well that night.

. . .

The army on foot was challenged by the road to Saint Henri as well. Known as the Justinian Road, after a French missionary in the region, it was a morass of mud and snow. "The roads were very bad by means of the great rains and snows that had fallen – we most of the way waded half leg deep in the mud and water," recorded Abner Stocking. "We marched but 17 miles."[7] Dearborn, among the sick who were relegated to being transported by borrowed or hired canoe down the Chaudière, watched the marchers in sympathy. "Our men proceed'd down the River, tho[ugh], in poor Circumstances, for Travelling, a Great Number of them being Barefoot, and the Weather Cold and Snowy," he observed.[8] He was later to join them for the final leg of the marching once the road left the river's edge. Stocking, summing up the final miles of marching, wrote, "Our [clothes] were torn in pieces by the bushes and hung in strings – few of us had any shoes…and beards long and visages thin and meager. I thought we much resembled the animals which inhabit New-Spain, called the Ourang-Outang."[9] A sight they must have been indeed. I had felt a little like an orangutan myself at the end of my march. It's no wonder that so few Canadians signed on to the American cause.

Throughout, Arnold was hurrying out in front of the army, thinking one step ahead. Seeing that additional provisions and supplies were sent back for his men, he was simultaneously preparing for the battle ahead – sending out scouts to get information on manpower and armaments in Quebec, searching for boats to cross the Saint Lawrence, recruiting Frenchmen and American Indians to their cause, and a thousand other details.

Once reaching Saint Henri, the road closely paralleled the Etchemin River downstream to Pointe de Levy, jutting out into the Saint Lawrence. Covered in logs, this final leg of the journey was called the Pavement Road, so named because of the log cordurouy used to prevent the knee-deep mire found on the Justinian Road (one can find a similar construction technique on logging roads or snowmobile trails in the 21st century, though of course it has fallen out of fashion for pedestrian use). Their long walk through the woods was nearly at an end. Reaching Saint Henri near midnight, the army built roaring fires to warm their chilled bones and await further orders. The following day they proceeded more slowly, awaiting confirmation that no British barred the way to the Saint Lawrence (none did).

On November 8th, 1775, they finally advanced to within sight of the Saint Lawrence. "When we halted we were within sight of Quebec, the river St. Lawrence between us and the town," wrote George Morison, who then expressed sentiments that likely all were feeling. "We were filled with joy at this event, when we saw ourselves at the end of our destination; and at length freed from the misery we endured in the woods."[10] They had indeed borne a lot to escape the wilderness and arrive where they were. Now, with only one last obstacle in their way, they would soon be at the gates of Quebec City, ready to attempt to take it for the American colonies.

· · ·

I woke on my final morning of the trip to a cold drizzle. The first week in Maine had been bluebird skies, but I would finish in poor weather. Such is life.

After eating the last meal of the trip – oatmeal and coffee, of course – I hopped on the river for what would turn out to be one of the most exciting days of the journey. The lower Etchemin is densely populated with Class II and Class III rapids, which meant that I was challenged throughout, as few stretches of river on this journey had done to date.

The first couple I navigated without trouble, having to skirt the edges of larger waves and ease over small drops where, had I been in the center, I would have invariably swamped in the holes created at the base of the drops. The river presented as one large logistics problem, and I shook my head in glee once or twice as I overcame each set. What fun!

Where a day paddler or whitewater kayaker or canoer might risk all to go through a big wave or drop a large ledge, a long-distance tripper like myself risks little. With my food, gear, and existence in my canoe, a swim can mean that I might lose essential equipment or provisions. Even at this late date in the trip, with the take-out looming, I was not willing to risk losing anything. Skirting large rapids, and lining or portaging where necessary was the name of the game for me. But that didn't mean it wasn't enjoyable – it just meant that I'd save the crazed adrenaline rush for another day and instead get my joy from simply continuing to move onwards.

Soon I came to Etchemin Falls, a massive waterfall dropping forty or fifty feet precipitously. I could hear it from far away and as I approached it only grew louder. Passing under a railroad trestle, the river began to quicken. I hugged river right, edging my way downstream nearly to the top of the drop before finally stopping. I scouted the edge of the river, considering what would have likely been an ill-fated attempt to stay in the water and line the canoe over the falls before deciding that discretion was the better part of valor. I lined back upstream briefly to the railroad trestle and portaged quickly up the bank beneath to a riverside road.

The map showed no easy access back to the river below the falls so I walked along the road, hoping for inspiration. After a couple hundred yards I crossed a culvert whose flow led back to the river. I dropped the canoe and followed the stream on foot only to find it cascading down a vertical cliff wall to the Etchemin, now sixty feet below. Not a good put-in.

I reloaded up and continued on, finding another culvert soon after. The road bent away from the river just ahead so instead of scouting I simply started down the stream fully loaded, with an 'Etchemin or bust' attitude, skirting a farmer's field and walking in the flow.

As I neared the river, the field disappeared and scraggly bushes took over. Soon, this stream too began to drop quickly, in an effort to rejoin the main river. But instead of one vertical cliff face, it was several, shorter vertical earth faces. Weighing my options, I went for it.

To descend the wall with the canoe, I took it off my shoulders and placed it on the ground. Holding onto the bow line, I lowered it hand over hand nearly vertically until it lodged in a small outcropping of brush. Then, hoping it wouldn't budge, I too descended next to the boat, rappelling down the bank with the help of some of the brush eking out an existence on the steep wall. And repeated. It went surprisingly smoothly and after three iterations of lowering the canoe and then lowering myself, I finally reached the level of the river and was able to put in again, very pleased with myself. I'm quite sure that that has never been used previously as a put-in, nor do I suspect that my first descent will lead to a wave of future users. But it worked.

Two additional portages appeared, both around shorter, five to seven foot ledges. On one I easily followed an ATV trail on river left and the next I knit together a route through a network of herd paths. Seemingly interminable and without destination, it was clear that dozens of people were skirting the riverbank here in and among the rock outcroppings that peppered the area. Tracing routes up and down steep hillocks and ridges, they sometimes seemed to simply disappear into the brush. Other times they lopped back in on themselves, creating several endless loops. Whoever had made them used them frequently for the earth was beaten down and no vegetation grew in the routes. And interspersed along these herd paths were wooden and metal shanties.

As I tried to navigate along the twisting paths, I couldn't help but admire the construction of these humble abodes. With four walls and a roof on most, they were all clearly made of *very* recycled materials. Scraps of plywood, plasterboard, corrugated iron, plastic, and even the occasional cinderblock or stack of bricks all contributed to their design. It was a hodge-podge of materials. But it was also clear that some time had been put into making sure they were strongly built, and there was even some rough aesthetic value to many. Painted various colors, or sometimes simply taking their tone from the original colors of the materials, they were perched in picturesque settings, sometimes atop short cliffs overlooking the heavy rapids I was circumnavigating. I even set down the canoe twice to get a closer look at them; at one point carefully enjoying a short cantilevered deck that looked out over the river from twenty feet up (I wasn't *that* confident about their sound engineering). On this morning, all were deserted, making me feel like I was portaging through an eerie ghost town. Whether built by kids or folks down on their luck, they were rough shelters sitting in a beautiful spot.

I continued my slow way down the Etchemin, portaging an additional two times a short distance over rocks along the river's edge to avoid short drops. Then, without warning, I rounded a corner to the right and there, spread before me in the misty haze, was the Saint Lawrence River. Through the soupy fog I could see the distant shore. Quebec at last! I drifted for a while, simply looking out at the river that I had been working towards for the past two weeks. In spite of the weather, it was a beautiful sight.

The Etchemin dropped one last time, directly into the Saint Lawrence and I portaged over some final rocks into the larger river. Feeling joy, peace, serenity, and a slight disappointment that the trip was ending, I wondered if Arnold felt similarly upon sighting the river himself. I suspect he found mostly relief mixed with worried anticipation of the fight to come. But I also suspect, that he, like myself, found some pride in having successfully come all that distance from Colburn's Boatyard in Maine. It had been quite a journey for both of us.

·   ·   ·

Pointe de Levy was the scene of bustling activity for the invading Americans. Examining their provisions, ammunition, arms, and other equipment, Arnold found them unsurprisingly lacking. Much had been lost on the march and the Americans were down to only a few rounds of ammunition per man (Centuries later, Duluth Wing would find some of the lost supplies along the route, as described above). One of the largest chores was therefore to re-outfit the army into a well-supplied fighting force.

Near the mouth of the Etchemin rested a small building known as Caldwell's Mill. The British had neglected to destroy it, perhaps because it was owned by a high-ranking official, and the Americans found a good supply of flour within. As stragglers daily joined the camp, the army drilled regularly to regain its discipline and streamline its maneuvers. The men were kept busy repairing clothing and gear and constructing ladders to scale the walls of Quebec.

Others were dispatched to round up all available water craft. Upon learning of the Americans' arrival, the leaders at Quebec had ordered that "all the canoes, boats, shallops & craft shou'd be brought off from the opposite shore & from the Island of Orleans."[11] This would prove to be no obstacle for the intrepid Americans. They spread out into the hinterlands in search of navigable craft and returned with enough canoes and dories to get the army across the Saint Lawrence. Thayer tells a humorous (at least to later-day readers) anecdote regarding his and Return Meigs' search for craft. "Major Meigs met me at St. Marys...in order to purchase canoes." Thayer then remembers Meigs' disappearing act when it came time to actually transport the boats to where they were needed. "Then Major Meigs left me, whom I never saw since, and [we] had to carry [the canoes] 30 miles on our Backs, 4 men under each canoe to Point Levi."[12] For Meigs' part, he simply stated "I was on business"[13] in his journal that day, seemingly preferring not to note in detail his escape from hard labor. Thayer must have shaken his head in disgust at Meigs' effrontery, but in the end the canoes got to where they were needed.

The men waiting at Point Levy were not idle. An ill-advised scouting expedition by the British resulted in the capture of a young midshipman who was left behind when the scouts were discovered. He made an attempt to swim for it upon discovery which nearly cost him his life when a homicidal American Indian scout swam after him and caught him. Cooler heads prevailed and he was made a prisoner of war. Others continued with preparation for the crossing of the river and subsequent anticipated assault on the walls of Quebec.

On the afternoon of November 13th, Arnold called a council of war. "Two Men of war Lying in the river Between Point-levi, and Quebec, and Guard Boats passing all night, up and Down the River,"[14] barred the way, as Dearborn noted, but they decided to move forward with the crossing that very day, regardless of the obstacles. Meigs describes the evening's events. "At nine o'clock, we began to embark our men on board 35 canoes, and at 4 o'clock in the morning we got over and landed about 500 men, entirely undiscovered."[15] With greased and muffled oarlocks and paddles, the men made their way across the river, some passing *between* the two men-of-war, amazingly without being detected. Not only that, but it took three trips to get the 500 men across, meaning that they passed the guard ships at least five times. It must have been a harrowing journey.

The crossing was not without incident, however. One group was partway across when disaster struck, with "one of the birch canoes bursting asunder in the midst of the St. Lawrence,"¹⁶ Senter writes. Luckily, no one perished but they lost their guns and equipment.

Dawn began to break on the morning of the 14th as the third wave was finishing their crossing. It was decided that the remainder on the south shore – mostly the sick and infirm – would wait to cross at a later date. The men who had successfully landed alit in Wolfe's Cove, named for the British general who had landed there a short sixteen years prior during his own successful attack on Quebec. Arnold had decided to use the same route to the city's protective walls. At Wolfe's Cove, the waiting men built a large fire to warm up and dry out after the crossing. Unfortunately, as Senter tells us, it was noted by a patrol. "The fire was spied by one of the patrolling barges, who came towards shore." It was hailed by some of the men in an attempt to capture it and prevent their being known, but the boat heaved off. The Americans fired on it, wounding some, but it escaped to the city to give the news of the American's arrival at the shores of Quebec City. It was of no matter. The army had landed on the north shore of the Saint Lawrence, at the foot of the walls of Quebec City.

Three hundred miles and nearly eight weeks later, the invading army led by Benedict Arnold arrived at the gates of Quebec City from Maine. It was a journey fraught with peril and disaster, but a journey that had been successfully completed. As Arnold ground ashore after crossing the St. Lawrence River, he must have at least felt a modicum of gratitude for their arrival. But their greatest challenge still awaited them: the assault of Quebec City.

. . .

My own assault on Quebec was less climactic. I simply needed to arrive in one piece. I too had to cross the Saint Lawrence. And, while I had no need to muffle my oarlocks or paddle in darkness to evade defenders, I, like Arnold, would be dodging much larger ships than my own as well. Or so I'd been warned.

The Saint Lawrence River hosts tens of millions of tons of cargo annually, most on large container ships. These ships ply its water back and forth, year round, traveling between American and Canadian ports and the rest of the world. The Saint Lawrence drains all the Great Lakes, Lake Champlain, and hundreds of other smaller lakes into one of the largest estuaries in the world. To say the least, it is a formidable river. And although I would be crossing it at one of its narrowest points, it was still nearly a mile wide.

I had sought advice on the crossing from several sources. Parker and Frank had laughingly recounted their own crossing. "We would guess whether to speed up or slow down, to avoid the container ships. They sure were not going to stop or swerve to avoid our tiny canoe – it's a good thing we guessed right!" Several friends who had crossed nearby as part of a different canoe expedition gave similar stories. "Be careful," was their main piece of advice. And my father made me promise to call him upon successfully making it across so he would know I was okay – I could hear the trepidation in his voice when we had talked earlier that morning. I promised to him that I'd wait if the weather was bad.

It was foggy and overcast as I floated near shore, contemplating the open water in front of me – but the weather wasn't bad enough to hold me up. I did, after all, have a warm bed and food waiting for me in the city. My safety preparations were not exactly OSHA-approved. I stuck my spare paddle upright in the stern and duct-taped an orange T-shirt to it, as a sort of flag. It hung there a little forlornly in the still air. But it would have to do. And I contemplated wearing a headlamp as a beacon, but decided that it would be ineffective at best. Besides, I reasoned, if it came to it, I could jump out at the last second as my little craft was sliced in two by a larger ship. After all, I had seen that very technique tried in numerous action films – it always seemed to work for the hero.

For all the build-up, the crossing was a let-down in terms of dodging danger. I spotted not one ship, yacht, motorboat or dinghy between shoving off from the south shore and touching down in Wolfe's Cove. What a disappointment! I kept a continued lookout throughout the first half of the crossing – getting more nervous as I neared the midpoint of the river. "They'll be coming at any second," I kept telling myself. "Be ready!". But they never came. I drifted for a bit at what I estimated as the halfway point, snapping pictures of the bridges nearby and the shore in front of me. It didn't take long to make the trip – the current appeared to be negligible here and the wind was down due to the fog. Small waves lapped against the gunwales and all in all it turned out to be a pleasant paddle.

I touched ashore briefly at Wolfe's Cove. No longer as Arnold found it, it is built up with the usual trappings of a modern riverside. Besides, while Arnold finished his journey here, mine had a few more miles in it.

Quebec City harbor is four miles downstream and the paddle there from Wolfe's Cove was discouraging. Ample proof abounded along the shores that I had emerged from the countryside into an industrial city. The thick forests and pleasant farmlands that had lined the shores of my previous two weeks of paddling now definitively gave way to factories and smokestacks. The occasional oil slick again adorned the water's surface. Fighting a slight incoming tide did not help the situation. I made the best of it, however, waving to passersby along the river edge and absorbing it all. Arnold would have been surprised to see the change, of that I was sure.

The harbor – at least the one for smaller pleasure craft – is guarded by a lock that allows boats to come and go in spite of the tide changes. I rounded the final corner to find the lock's closed doors appear in front of me. A small office perched above the lock, its tinted windows clearly housing the lock operator. A small sign to the right, above a miniature traffic light, read, "Attendez the feu vert." So I waited, floating peacefully in my canoe, for the red light to change to green.

Five minutes passed, then another five, then ten more. The light did not change. The tinted windows glared implacably back at me as if to say, "You're no pleasure craft. You do not belong here." But I stared back. I've made use of several locks in previous travels and I was not about to give up on this one.

After nearly half an hour, however, the issue was taken from my hands. The lock operator finally emerged from her tinted castle and descended from her lordly perch. "Canoes are not permitted," she said in passable English. My appearance must have been a giveaway that I was not a local. Or perhaps my obvious obliviousness to lock protocol was the clue. "I've come a long way to use this lock," I responded, giving her my winningest grin. To no avail. She shrugged her shoulders, stating eloquently if incorrectly that it was out of her hands. It was clearly very much within her power to let me through but I chose not to press the issue and instead took out at a slip nearby. My journey had come to an abrupt end.

Chapter 12: Quebec City

"Surely a miracle must have been wrought in their favor. It is an undertaking above the common race of men, in this debauched age. They have traveled through woods and bogs, over precipices for the space of one hundred and twenty miles [sic], attended with every inconvenience and difficulty, to be surmounted only by men of indefatigable zeal and industry."[1] *– A Quebec citizen*

  A small picnic table overlooked the harbor and with gulls screeching through gray, clouded skies, I hauled my canoe and gear up to it and sat down. I felt like I deserved the rest. Three hundred miles of paddling and portaging is not something to shake a stick at.
  The table was adjacent to the lock and I watched it enviously as it opened and closed several times for two sailboats. The final remains of my food – two peanut butter and jelly sandwiches – were not what I had had in mind for a celebratory meal, but they were near at hand so I ate them hungrily and observed the goings on of the city. The harbor-side seemed a popular spot for running and jogging, and most stared curiously at me as they moved past. Dressed in dirty clothes with a large pack and canoe on the ground next to me, I could not have been a typical sight.
  But I didn't say much. It was very pleasant to simply sit there and relax. Only mid-morning, I had nowhere to be and the Saint Lawrence spread before me was a splendid backdrop for my musings.
  I had completed Arnold's journey, 238 years after he too had arrived in Quebec. While the obstacles had changed and the scenery too, it was still a formidable challenge and I swelled slightly with a pride as I thought about the journey, about all the upstream miles logged, portages completed, and rapids successfully navigated. Not knowing that I was capable of such a solo journey at the beginning, I now felt like I could conquer the world.
  But it was more than just the physical aspects of the trip. Reading Arnold's men's journals by headlamp each night meant that I hadn't been doing it alone. I had had 600 companions on the trip, with whom to compare notes with, empathize with over long portages, and revel with in the successful navigation of rapids and waterfalls. Far from being a solitary experience, instead I had made

the trip as part of a large expedition. The several centuries of separation compressed into nothing as I laughed at their jokes, shook my head in compassion over their miseries, and shared their anguish as my own feet blistered beneath me and I too faced the river's implacable power. Yes, I didn't face hunger or imminent death – modern maps, equipment and the simple expansion of the 'civilized world' had made those challenges largely irrelevant – but in almost every other way I too had joined them for the successes and failures of the trip. I felt a certain arrogance, as I'm sure they had as well, to have overcome it all. I think we all strutted a little bit on the Quebec shore, with our chests out, shoulders back, and chins held just a little bit higher. But whereas my appearance at Quebec would be a mere anticlimax, an afterthought to the journey itself, Arnold had barely begun. He had arrived at his objective; now the real work began.

. . .

Arnold arrived on the northern shore of the Saint Lawrence River on November 14th, 1775. Upon reaching Wolfe's Cove the army marched up to the Plains of Abraham – a vast expanse of farming and grazing lands outside the city. From here they would stage their attack. Rumors later circulated that the gates to the city stood open that day, although they were never confirmed. They may well have, given total British surprise upon finding that the Americans had made it across the river – the Brits were sure that they were safe due to the removal of all watercraft from the south side of the river combined with the two warships stationed in the channel.

A hurried conference ensued among the American officers. Due to a combination of the total lack of information about the city, exhaustion of the just-crossed troops, and a lack of siege equipment which had been left behind, the decision was made to not assault the city in the early morning hours. Many historians agree that this was an ill-informed decision, for surprise was on their side and it likely would have provided their best shot at success. A further fateful decision was made days later to prolong the delay and await General Montgomery. Montgomery was leading an additional 300 men and represented the second prong of the attack on Quebec City. He had taken Montreal in mid-November and would join Arnold outside Quebec in early December.

The British and Americans proceeded to skirmish throughout the coming weeks, with both weapons and words. But not until December 31st (many soldiers' enlistments were up the following day) in the midst of a blizzard did they attack Quebec in full. Bitter fighting ensued in which Montgomery was killed and Arnold wounded. The loss of their leaders combined with confusion due to the nighttime attack and blizzard conditions would prove to be their undoing. The assault eventually sputtered with most Americans becoming either casualties or captives.* It would be several more months before the siege, such as it was, was given up by the army's remnants, but most knew that the failure on New Year's Eve presaged doom for a successful campaign. It was a pitiable end to a heroic effort.

In spite of the failure to take the city, Arnold would be hailed as a hero. Having traveled through the "howling wilderness,"[2] his men appeared to be near death. Adorned in, at best, filthy, torn clothing, often with no shoes on their feet, their skinny, haggard faces could not have filled observers with the sense of a conquering army. Arnold himself described them as "almost naked and in want of every necessity."[3]

Yet their appearance belied their drive. Slowly recuperating on the Plains of Abraham, the legend of their exploits traveled quickly. Even the British were impressed, one captain calling them "the Flower of the rebel army."[4] Another was amazed at the depths of their endurance, noting that they seemed to be possessed of "indefatigable zeal and industry."[5] And acclaim soon spread further. Americans back home in the colonies named Arnold an "American Hannibal," and his men "famine-proof veterans."[6] Another lauded the expedition as "equal[ling] Xenophons Retreat from Persia…nothing greater has been done since the Days of Alexander."[7]

Arnold would go on to further adventures, achieving even more fame for the role he played in the Battle of Saratoga where he was described as "inspired with the fury of a demon," and "the very genius of war,"[8] descriptors that equally describe his exploits in Maine and Quebec. But the laurels would all be stripped from him when he tried to turn West Point over to the British later in the war. Dying in London in 1801, his name lives on today as a synonym for treachery while his earlier deeds often going unrecognized or under-valued.† Arriving successfully at Quebec City in 1775 may well have been the high point of his career.

. . .

---

* A highly interesting addendum to the expedition is provided by Simon Fobes. Taken captive during the assault, he later escaped with two others and retraced the expedition's route back up the Chaudière and down the Kennebec. Passing the remains of deceased soldiers, they re-experienced some of the same hardships endured on the original journey. Arriving back at his home in September, 1776, he nonchalantly took a seat just inside the door. His mother "gave me a look, then resumed her work, but said nothing, thinking me some straggler that had called in for food or drink or the like." (Roberts, *March*, p. 613). It would take his little sister to recognize him, his travels and experiences having so remarkably changed his visage.

† Aaron Burr, later vice-president under Thomas Jefferson and another member of the expedition also bears the dubious distinction of being one of the most famous traitors to the United States. Still more coincidentally, the third most famous traitor of the era, General James Wilkinson, was stationed nearby at St. Johns soon after in May, 1776. What was it about Canada in those days?!

As I sat musing over the expedition and its members, one passerby's curiosity finally got the best of her. Introducing herself as Julie, she asked just what I thought I was doing sitting on a bench with a canoe next to me.

"That's how I got here! I paddled it here from Maine," I laughingly replied, enjoying the dubious expression that crept onto her face. I explained Arnold's trip – remember that the Quebecois are generally less informed about the expedition than Mainers – and gave her a quick overview of my travels.

"Where are you going now? Is someone coming to pick you up? How are you getting home?" She seemed genuinely worried about my future.

"I'm here in the city for the next two days. I want to see the Plains of Abraham where Arnold camped, and the city walls. I'm staying at a hostel downtown. I'm not actually really sure how to get there." I had a map of the city with me, but anyone who has been to Quebec City's Lower Town knows that the narrow streets twist and wind back upon themselves as they ascend and descend the steep hillside. I was a little nervous about my ability to navigate them beneath a canoe.

"I'll show you," she said shyly but matter-of-factly. Clearly a cautious, introspective woman, she nonetheless gave up whatever plans she had for the next half hour to take me to where I needed to go. Her look of compassion and complete lack of guile immediately won me over, and I accepted with alacrity. After all, I needed her help.

So we set out. She had a bike with her and she walked beside it, leading the way. I followed with my pack on my back and the canoe on my shoulders, just like every other portage I had made on the trip. Except this time it was through downtown Quebec. Tourists and locals alike gawked as we walked past, snapping pictures and pointing. Self-consciously but resolutely she continued onwards, a little embarrassed at the spectacle we were making while I grinned and waved at onlookers behind her, thoroughly enjoying the attention.

So led by a kind-hearted woman, I succeeded where Arnold had not. I made it into the heart of Lower Town – Arnold's goal that New Year's Eve so many years ago. In the following days I toured the city, enjoying its sights and sounds and visiting many of the places associated with the American assault on the city. But the trip for me culminated in that march through downtown. I had paddled three hundred miles from Maine to Quebec, following Arnold's route. It was a powerful moment, tramping along the cobblestone streets. They have been there since Arnold's time and my feet may well have trod in the same places as some of the American soldiers' as they fought so desperately in the snow. It was a perfect way for me to wrap up the experience.

We arrived at the hostel and Julie turned to face me. "Here we are," she said.

"Yes, indeed." I answered. "Here we are. Thanks. Thanks a lot." I had made it. I had conquered Quebec.

Acknowledgements

In taking this journey and writing this book, I of course rely heavily on the journals and memoirs of the men who made the trip (so far no journal by one of the few women who traveled with them has come to light). Many thanks to Kenneth Roberts for compiling and publishing many of them in an out-of-print but still easily found book, March to Quebec. I also pored over many of his papers and notes currently stored in Rauner Special Collections at Dartmouth College Library in Hanover, NH for additional sources and notes.

I made use of secondary sources as well, many of which helped to translate the sometimes indecipherable, cryptic, and often contradictory or biased journal entries. In particular Justin Smith's Arnold's March from Cambridge to Quebec was a valuable volume and a joy to read due to his peculiarly intimate narrative style.* Thomas Desjardin's Through a Howling Wilderness, Stephen Clark's Following Their Footsteps, Stephen Darley's Voices From A Wilderness Expedition and Arthur Lefkowitz's Benedict Arnold's Army are also valuable works of non-fiction and remain in print. I used all of these books to both help research 1775 memoirists and as sources of background for the broader historical picture. I am indebted to them all for their research efforts.

Personal thanks are also due to many people. First, I owe a debt of gratitude to Parker and Frank. They were two of the six-man expedition who replicated much of the trip in 1973. Taking time from their busy schedules, they met with me on several occasions to share their experience. Their tales of rapids, log drives, and disaster not only eerily mimicked some of the same hurdles Arnold faced but also spurred me onwards to make the trip.

---

*An example of Smith's style and narrative tone: "[Montresor] accomplished his task, drew a map, and wrote a journal. Later the map and an imperfect draft of the journal fell into the hands of Benedict Arnold; and later still they both fall into ours. In the course of our inquiries we shall very probably need to consult them." Justin Harvey Smith, *Arnold's March From Cambridge to Quebec: A Critical Study, Together with a Reprint From Arnold's Journal*, p. 17

Thank you very much John and Patty for putting me up for the night and feeding me such a splendid dinner. Welcoming my smelly self into your home after a week on the water without so much as batting an eye could not have been easy! A similar thanks is due to Uncle Chuck and Aunt Diane for another night of hospitality. Your welcome was a great way to start out the trip.

Thanks to Julie for guiding me through the streets of Quebec. I hope I didn't embarrass you too much, and good luck with whatever comes next for you.

To Sarah, who has driven me home from several trips now, you are wonderful support for my travels. Road-tripping with you is always a delight. Your thoughts and feedback on my writing are always appreciated, as are those from Peg, Mary, Sue and Elizabeth.

And to my girlfriend, Elizabeth, who not only dropped me off at the Colburn House but who has provided support throughout. You are a wellspring of positivity and enthusiasm. Without your loving sustenance, I'm not sure where I'd be.

Finally, a special thank you goes out to Duluth Wing. He made the trip in segments in the early 1970's himself and since then has been discovering artifacts along the route and maintaining portage trails, not to mention being very active in the small but vibrant organization, the Arnold Expedition Historical Society. He lived along the route, met me for breakfast mid-trip and gave me a tour of his treasure trove of Arnold artifacts before waving me on my way up the Dead River. His wife packed me a bag of sweets before I continued on. Sadly, he passed a few months after that meeting and the Arnold-enthusiast community lost a dear and avid member. It is to him this book is dedicated.

Notes

Introduction
1. Smith, *Arnold's March*, p. 2
2. Arthur S. Lefkowitz, *Benedict Arnold's Army*, p. 214
3. Thomas A. Desjardin, *Through A Howling Wilderness*, p. 189
4. Ibid., p. 96
5. Moses Kimball, unpublished manuscript, p. 6
6. Ibid., p. 4-6
7. Kenneth Roberts, *March to Quebec*, p. xi-xii
8. Lefkowitz, *Arnold's Army*, p. 264
9. Lefkowitz, *Arnold's Army*, p. 192

Historical Background
1. Roberts, *March*, p. 299
2. Lefkowitz, *Arnold's Army*, p. 59
3. Smith, *Arnold's March*, p. 5

Chapter 1: Planning the March
1. Lefkowitz, *Arnold's Army*, p. 101
2. Bruce Hertz, "Michigan six trace Arnold's Trail," *Bangor Daily News 08/03/1973*, Accessed 03/16/2014, http://news.google.com/newspapers?nid=2457&dat=19730803&id=8KxAAAAAIBAJ&sjid=WjgHAAAAIBAJ&pg=3229,835023
3. Smith, *Arnold's March*, p. 76
4. Lefkowitz, *Arnold's Army*, p. 80
5. Smith, *Arnold's March*, p. 75
6. Ibid., p. 77
7. Ibid., p. 56
8. Lefkowitz, *Arnold's Army*, p. 160
9. Ibid., p. 214
10. Roberts, *March*, p. 545

Interlude: Who Were They?
1. Roberts, *March*, p. 505
2. Michael Stephenson, *Patriot Battles*, p. 80
3. Roberts, *March*, p. 303
4. Ibid., p. 505
5. Lefkowitz, *Arnold's Army*, p. 268

Chapter 2: Setting Out
1. Lefkowitz, *Arnold's Army*, p. 57
2. Ibid., p. 56
3. Ibid., p. 57
4. Ibid., p. 58
5. Roberts, *March*, p. 512
6. Smith, *Arnold's March*, p. 62
7. Desjardin, *Howling Wilderness*, p. 21
8. Lefkowitz, *Arnold's Army*, p. 76
9. Roberts, *March*, p. 303
10. Ibid., p. 132

Interlude: The Bateaux – Their Construction and Navigation
1. Smith, *Arnold's March*, p. 78
2. Desjardin, *Howling Wilderness*, p. 13
3. Smith, *Arnold's March*, p. 100
4. Roberts, *March*, p. 199
5. Desjardin, *Howling Wilderness*, p. 60
6. Ibid., p. 25
7. Smith, *Arnold's March*, p. 79
8. Desjardin, *Howling Wilderness*, p. 60
9. Roberts, *March*, p. 202
10. Ibid., p. 201
11. Ibid., p. 72
12. Lefkowitz, *Arnold's Army*, p. 107
13. Desjardin, *Howling Wilderness*, p. 60
14. Ibid.
15. Roberts, *March*, p. 518
16. Ibid., p. 582
17. Ibid., p. 550

Chapter 3: The Lower Kennebec
1. Desjardin, *Howling Wilderness*, p. 60
2. Roberts, *March*, p. 69

3. Ibid., p. 250
4. Ibid., p. 132
5. Ibid., p. 250
6. Ibid., p. 132
7. Ibid., p. 304
8. Smith, *Arnold's March*, p. 101
9. Roberts, *March*, p. 201
10. Ibid., p. 520
11. Desjardin, *Howling Wilderness*, p. 61
12. Stephen Clark, *Following Their Footsteps*, p. 33
13. Roberts, *March*, p. 251
14. Ibid., p. 548
15. Ibid., p. 46
16. Ibid., p. 251
17. Ibid., p. 133
18. Ibid., p. 548
19. William Dorr, *Descendants of Edward Dorr*, Accessed 03/20/2014, http://www.gencircles.com/users/cdorr/1/data/959
20. Roberts, *March*, p. 251
21. Ibid., p. 549

Interlude: Their Gear – What They Carried and Wore
1. Desjardin, *Howling Wilderness*, p. 38
2. Lefkowitz, *Arnold's Army*, p. 82-83; Smith 100-101
3. Desjardin, *Howling Wilderness*, p. 54-55
4. Ibid., p. 19
5. Roberts, *March*, p. 176

Chapter 4: The Upper Kennebec
1. Roberts, *March*, p. 72
2. Ibid., p. 47
3. Ibid., p. 203
4. Ibid., p. 177
5. Ibid., p. 549
6. Ibid., p. 252
7. Ibid., p. 49
8. Ibid.
9. Ibid.
10. Ibid., p. 19

Interlude: What Did They Eat?
1. Roberts, *March*, p. 440

2. Desjardin, *Howling Wilderness*, p. 14
3. Roberts, *March*, p. 417
4. Ibid., p. 436
5. Ibid., p. 207
6. Stephen Darley, *Voices From A Wilderness Expedition*, p. 177
7. Roberts, *March*, p. 253
8. Desjardin, *Howling Wilderness*, p. 66
9. Ibid., p. 36
10. Roberts, *March*, p. 51
11. Ibid., p. 307
12. Ibid., p. 315
13. Roberts, *March*, p. 324-325

Chapter 5: The Great Carrying Place
1. Roberts, *March*, p. 309-310
2. Ibid., p. 214
3. Ibid., p. 308
4. Ibid., p. 19
5. Ibid.
6. Roberts, *March*, p. 513-514
7. Ibid., p. 622
8. Ibid., p. 623
9. Ibid., p. 205
10. Ibid., p. 73
11. Smith, *Arnold's March*, p. 125
12. Roberts, *March* p. 134
13. Ibid., p. 257
14. Desjardin, *Howling Wilderness*, p. 47
15. Roberts, *March*, p. 74
16. Ibid., p. 327
17. Ibid., p. 50
18. Ibid., p. 70
19. Ibid., p. 207

Interlude: In Sickness and In Health
1. Roberts, *March*, p. 136
2. Ibid., p. 218
3. Ibid., p. 311
4. Ibid., p. 200
5. Ibid., p. 205-206
6. Ibid., p. 44
7. Ibid., p. 218

8. Ibid., p. 145
9. Ibid., p. 311
10. Ibid., p. 521
11. Ibid., p. 218
12. Lefkowitz, *Arnold's Army*, p. 235
13. Ibid., p. 234
14. Ibid., p. 235

Chapter 6: The Lower Dead River (Flagstaff Lake)
1. Roberts, *March*, p. 52
2. Ibid., p. 70-71
3. Ibid., p. 72
4. Ibid., p. 206-207
5. Ibid., p. 551
6. Ibid.
7. Ibid., p. 550-551
8. Ibid., p. 178
9. Ibid., p. 52
10. Ibid., p. 136
11. Ibid., p. 254
12. Ibid., p. 53
13. Ibid., p. 314
14. Ibid.
15. Ibid.
16. Ibid., p. 476
17. Ibid., p. 330
18. Ibid., p. 54
19. Ibid., p. 208

Interlude: The Expedition's Interactions with American Indians
1. Roberts, *March*, p. 80-81
2. Smith, *Arnold's March*, p. 82
3. Roberts, *March*, p. 345
4. Ibid., p. 70
5. Ibid., p. 51
6. Ibid., p. 82
7. Ibid., p. 83
8. Ibid., p. 447
9. Ibid., p. 254
10. Ibid., p. 344
11. Ibid., p. 86
12. Ibid., p. 60-61

13. Ibid., p. 221
14. Ibid., p. 345
15. Ibid., p. 323

Chapter 7: The North Branch of the Dead River and the Chain of Ponds
1. Roberts, *March*, p. 55
2. Ibid., p. 54-55
3. Ibid., p. 209
4. Ibid., p. 179
5. Lefkowitz, *Arnold's Army*, p. 141
6. Roberts, *March*, p. 208
7. Ibid., p. 180
8. Ibid., p. 209
9. Ibid., p. 56-57
10. Ibid., p. 210
11. Ibid.
12. Ibid., p. 476
13. Ibid., p. 258
14. Ibid., p. 75
15. Ibid., p. 258
16. Ibid., p. 56
17. Ibid., p. 75
18. Ibid., p. 517
19. Ibid., p. 256-257
20. Ibid., p. 257
21. Ibid.
22. Ibid., p. 211
23. Ibid., p. 552
24. Ibid., p. 58
25. Ibid., p. 522
26. Ibid., p. 316
27. Ibid., p. 56-57
28. Ibid., p. 57
29. Ibid., p. 180
30. Ibid., p. 213
31. Ibid.
32. Ibid., p. 553
33. Ibid., p. 521
34. Ibid., p. 213

Interlude: What Did They Do For Fun?
1. Roberts, *March*, p. 516

2. Ibid., p. 514
3. Ibid., p. 342
4. Ibid., p. 312
5. Ibid., p. 514
6. Ibid., p. 582
7. Ibid., p. 310
8. Ibid., p. 134
9. Ibid., p. 333
10. Ibid., p. 332
11. Ibid., p. 514
12. Ibid., p. 262
13. Ibid., p. 474
14. Ibid., p. 308-309
15. Ibid., p. 319
16. Ibid., p. 316
17. Ibid., p. 342

Chapter 8: The Height of Land
1. Roberts, *March*, p. 522-523
2. Ibid., p. 77
3. Ibid., p. 137
4. Ibid.
5. Ibid., p. 523
6. Ibid., p. 335-336
7. Ibid., p. 553
8. Ibid., p. 214
9. Ibid., p. 258
10. Ibid., p. 524
11. Ibid., p. 316
12. Ibid., p. 522-523
13. Ibid., p. 137
14. Lefkowitz, *Arnold's Army*, p. 164
15. Roberts, *March*, p. 215
16. Ibid., p. 552
17. Ibid., p. 215
18. Ibid., p. 79
19. Ibid.

Interlude: The Women of Arnold's Army
1. Roberts, *March*, p. 338
2. Much of the preceding two paragraphs was culled from Lefkowitz, *Arnold's Army*, p. 52

3. Roberts, *March*, p. 546
4. Ibid., p. 184-185
5. Patricia Bigelow, *The Bigelow Family Genealogy*, p. 73-75, Accessed 04/01/2014, https://archive.org/stream/bigelowfamilygen01bige#page/72/mode/2up 5/2/13
6. Lefkowitz, *Arnold's Army*, p. 165
7. Roberts, *March*, p. 336
8. Ibid., p. 337
9. Ibid., p. 556
10. Darley, *Voices*, p. 167
11. Roberts, *March*, p. 483
12. Ibid., p. 494

Chapter 9: The Arnold River and Lac Megantic
1. Roberts, *March*, p. 217
2. Ibid., p. 58
3. Ibid., p. 59
4. Much of this paragraph comes from research discussed by Smith, *Arnold's March*, p. 203-210
5. Roberts, *March*, p. 138
6. Ibid., p. 438
7. Ibid., p. 554
8. Ibid., p. 217
9. Ibid., p. 583
10. Ibid., p. 526
11. Ibid., p. 217

Interlude: What Kept Them Going?
1. Roberts, *March*, p. 528
2. Ibid., p. 51
3. Ibid., p. 78
4. Ibid., p. 327
5. Ibid., p. 521
6. Ibid., p. 528
7. Ibid., p. 341-342
8. Ibid., p. 526
9. Ibid., p. 439
10. Desjardin, *Howling Wilderness*, p. 79

Chapter 10: The Upper Chaudière
1. Roberts, *March*, p. 338

2. Ibid., p. 555
3. Ibid., p. 218
4. Ibid., p. 60
5. Ibid., p. 340
6. Roberts, *March*, p. 338
7. Ibid., p. 219
8. Ibid., p. 555
9. Ibid., p. 141
10. Ibid., p. 441
11. Ibid., p. 341
12. Ibid., p. 218
13. Ibid., p. 377
14. Ibid., p. 318
15. Mathias Ogden, *Journal of Mathias Ogden on the March to Quebec with Benedict Arnold 1775*, p. 2-3, Accessed 03/17/2014, http://www.arnoldsmarch.com/research/Eyewitness_Accounts/mathias_ogden.pdf
16. Lefkowitz, *Arnold's Army*, p. 172
17. Roberts, *March*, p. 555
18. Ibid., p. 585
19. Ibid., p. 532
20. Ibid., p. 258
21. Ibid., p. 213
22. Ibid., p. 219
23. Ibid., p. 139
24. Ibid., p. 216
25. Ibid., p. 181
26. Ibid., p. 608
27. Ibid., p. 61
28. Ibid., p. 219
29. Ibid., p. 140
30. Ibid., p. 556
31. Ibid., p. 343
32. Ibid., p. 585
33. Clark, *Following*, p. 85
34. Roberts, *March*, p. 478
35. Ibid., p. 556

Interlude: The Quebecois
1. Roberts, *March*, p. 82
2. Ibid., p. 58
3. Ibid., p. 531

4. Ibid., p. 346
5. Ibid., p. 557
6. Ibid., p. 140
7. Desjardin, *Howling Wilderness*, p. 109
8. Roberts, *March*, p. 346
9. Ibid., p. 262
10. Ibid., p. 250
11. Ibid., p. 557
12. Ibid.
13. Lefkowitz, *Arnold's Army*, p. 186

Chapter 11: The Lower Chaudière, Etchemin, and Saint Lawrence Rivers
1. Roberts, *March*, p. 223
2. Ibid., p. 222
3. Ibid., p. 181
4. Ibid., p. 223
5. Ibid., p. 141
6. Ibid., p. 6
7. Ibid., p. 557-558
8. Ibid., p. 140
9. Ibid., p. 558
10. Ibid., p. 531
11. Smith, *Arnold's March*, p. 455
12. Roberts, *March*, p. 262-263
13. Ibid., p. 181
14. Ibid., p. 141
15. Ibid., p. 182
16. Ibid., p. 225

Chapter 12: Quebec City
1. Desjardin, *Howling Wilderness*, p. 119
2. Roberts, *March*, p. 210
3. Ibid., p. 93
4. Lefkowitz, *Arnold's Army*, p. 262
5. Ibid., p.194
6. Ibid., p. 192
7. Ibid., p. 264
8. Desjardin, *Howling Wilderness*, p. 195

Bibliography

Books

Clark, Stephen. *Following Their Footsteps: A Travel Guide & History of the 1775 Secret Expedition to Capture Quebec.* Shapleigh, Me.: Clark Books, 2003.

Darley, Stephen. *Voices From A Wilderness Expedition: The Journals and Men of Benedict Arnold's Expedition to Quebec in 1775.* Bloomington, In.: AuthorHouse, 2011.

Desjardin, Thomas. *Through A Howling Wilderness.* New York: St. Martin's Press, 2006.

Lefkowitz, Arthur S. *Benedict Arnold's Army: The 1775 American Invasion of Canada During the Revolutionary War.* New York: Savas Beatie LLC, 2008.

Lossing, Benson John. *Our Country: A Household History For All Readers, From the Discovery of America to the Present Time, Volume 2.* New York: Johnson & Miles, 1878. pg. 821

Roberts, Kenneth. *March to Quebec.* New York: Doubleday, Doran & Company, Inc., 1938.

Smith, Justin Harvey. *Arnold's March From Cambridge to Quebec: A Critical Study, Together With A Reprint From Arnold's Journal.* New York: G. P. Putnam's Sons, 1903

Stephenson, Michael. *Patriot Battles: How the War of Independence Was Fought.* New York: HarperCollins Publishers, 2008.

Unpublished Manuscripts

Clark, Stephen. *Crisis in the Megantic Swamps: How the 1775 Expedition to Quebec Was Nearly Destroyed.* Copy of this essay was given to the author.

Foote, Fenner. Unpublished summary of expedition. Copy was accessed from Box 18, Folder 72 of the Kenneth Roberts Collection, Rauner Special Collections, Dartmouth College Library, Hanover, NH.

Kimball, Moses. Unpublished journal. Copy was accessed in Folder 775508.1, Rauner Special Collections, Dartmouth College Library, Hanover NH.

Websites

www.archive.org

www.arnoldsmarch.com

www.gencircles.com

www.hsccnh.org

http://news.google.com/newspapers?nid=3yMDF_cvnR8C

Image Credits

All 2013 Photographs of Author: Copyright 2013 by Sam Brakeley

Arnold Engraving: Accessed on 11/11/15 at: www.benedictarnold.org

Arnold's Expedition Across the Wilderness: Lossing, *Our Country*, p. 819

Journey Through The Wilderness: Lossing, *Our Country*, p. 821

Carrying The Bateaux At Skowhegan Falls: The Century illustrated monthly magazine. New York : The Century Co., 1903 Jan., p. 362. Accessed on 11/11/15 at: http://www.loc.gov/pictures/item/93509675/

Arnold's March To Quebec by Newell Convers Wyeth: Image accessed 11/11/15 at www.christies.com

Mural of Attack on Quebec Expedition: Image accessed 11/11/15 at www.massmemories.net

Made in the USA
Middletown, DE
01 December 2016